EDUCATE TO WIN

PATRICK MOURATOGLOU

– Clarisse, thank you for everything you give me every day: love, support, self-sacrifice. I know that I can always count on you. I also know the worth of everything you bring me, and that gives me the strength to be better.

– Raphaël, Juliette, and Charlotte, my three children, you are three extraordinary children. You are very different, but all three of you have this spark inside that makes you magnificent beings. I love you with all my heart and I am proud of you.

– To my parents who programmed me with love and devotion, I just want to say "thank you" for giving me so much. Mom, you have given all the love a mother can give to her children, and Dad, you gave me the image of success and the determination to achieve it.

– To Marcos Baghdatis, I want to thank you. Because of your accomplishments, because of what you have allowed me to share, because of your generosity, nothing will ever be the same…

Cover: Quatre
Cover photo: Denis Boulanger @ Amphora
Translated from the French by Vanessa Jacquemin

Interior: Amphora

© Éditions Amphora – December 2007
ISBN : 978-2-85180-**741**-0

EDUCATE TO WIN

PATRICK MOURATOGLOU

amphora sports
14, rue de l'Odéon – 75006 Paris

Forward

When I came up with the idea to write this book, I spoke to my acquaintances about it. I knew that the subject matter would appear shocking.

Yet my ten-year experience in the tennis world convinced me that champions are programmed at a very young age, and that their unique psychology makes them unique human beings who are capable of anything, who do not imagine limits and who are gifted with a formidable competitive spirit.

Two anecdotes made me decide to pursue this endeavour. They made me understand that I had to explain what was so obvious to me: a champion is first and foremost a unique psychological profile that is constructed at a very young age.

I had started working with Anastasia Pavlyuchenkova at the time. Anastasia is a 16-year-old Russian player who was crowned world junior champion at the age of 15. She has an intense competitive streak. She is a killer on the court.

We talked a lot, especially in the early days of our collaboration. I wanted to get to know her, to understand her and to know where she came from. She confided in me with these words:

"I'm very ambitious. I want to succeed in everything I do. I was brilliant in school, and I always wanted to be the best when it came to tennis. Ever since I was little, I've wanted to win every tournament I participated in. Incidentally, I won almost all of them. I participated in my first under-18 tournament at the age of 12. I advanced in the qualification rounds and then won the tournament. But I later learned that I didn't have the right to participate in this tournament. The rules specified that players weren't authorized to enter junior tournaments before the age of 13. I was therefore stripped of all the points I had won. I had to wait one year and start all over again. And I won again."

I admire above all the athlete in her, but I also like her unique personality, her unwavering confidence which is free of doubt, her incessant desire to win, and her commitment to her goals.

Nastia (her nickname) is a champion. A champion off the court who has been able to bring her fighting spirit onto the tennis court. This makes her a winner.

The second anecdote concerns a young, 16-year-old player competing in her age category at the French championships. She was playing her second round the day I discovered her. Her determination and originality impressed me. She played at the net and she literally "ate" her opponent with her attitude. I was starting off as a tennis agent at that time, and her enormous potential retained my attention. No one in the tennis world believed in her. The leading sports newspaper in France even printed the views of the director of the biggest sports management agency: "If Bartoli amounts to something in the future, I'll open a tobacco store." She became the French champion by the end of the week and at the end of the month, she won the second series criterium which propeled her to the No.20 spot in France. At the end of the year, she won the Orange Bowl in the under-16 category and became de facto one of the best female players in that age category. She rose to No.20 in the world a month after having participated in her first junior tournaments, and won the US Open Junior Championship eight months later. In July 2007 she reached the Wimbledon final against Venus Williams, after eliminating Justin

Henin in the semi-final and she now ranks No.11 in the world. What an accomplishment for someone people described as not very gifted and lacking in physical skills! What an accomplishment for someone who was ignored by the media all this time! Marion Bartoli has become the No.2 French player. She has accomplished what no one dared to imagine, but what she knew firmly in her heart. Ironically, I opened up the pages of the Journal du Dimanche the day of the final and stumbled upon an interview with Marion.

The headline? "I was programmed to win".

It was at that moment that I decided to make the leap. I have been training champions for ten years. I live amongst the best players in the world. I work with them and hang out with them.

These players are, above all else, human beings. I have always treated them as such, unlike many coaches who view them as ball-hitting machines. My entire system is founded on the idea that players bring their personality to the court, that if they are highly competitive, extremely strong and very confident human beings, they will only become better, and why not, greater champions.

In observing the effectiveness of my method, I realized that it was not unique to tennis but to every individual activity. If we can make humans more competitive and more capable of reaching their goals, if we know how to give them confidence in their abilities, then they will become more effective.

I think that my method can provide an interesting alternative to "traditional" education.

But these are not the only reasons that pushed me to write this book. Firstly, and especially at a time when sordid "scandals" tarnish the image of professional tennis, I want to offer a positive contribution to this sport that has given me so much. No, professional sport does not encourage extreme behavior. It is simply a reflection of our society. The image that it reflects back to us may not be as flattering as we would prefer, and that is why we criticize it.

Professional tennis, like other professional sports, is excessive and will remain so for it is inherent to the activity. It is therefore logical that the behavior of its members will also be excessive. Sports ethics and the law exist to force the sport to remain within acceptable limits. The excesses and illegal conduct described in these cases must be condemned with all the severity they deserve. They are unacceptable, but they do not reflect the sport, and therefore, damage its image.

Professional tennis is also a parable for life in all its glory: emotions, human journeys, values, a fight to succeed. It is the sublimation of one's own qualities and the dream for a better life. It is also the construction of a project with others: parents, children, coaches, and numerous supervisors. Professional tennis is filled with passion and tears but also with satisfaction and fullfilment. It is the ability for people to take great risks, to trust others, to invest themselves completely, and to question themselves. It is an opportunity for children to construct themselves differently through a life project, an activity, hope, around a new way of viewing education in a more specialized way, more focused, more restrictive, more responsible.

Professional tennis has given me a lot, and I hope to bring my own contribution to this sport through this book: to explain the factors which hinder or help a young player to become a champion.

The famous keys to success that everyone has been seeking for decades are finally available to each of us and are just waiting to be used. I want to give everyone the ability to obtain this from this book and to activate the tools themselves.

I want my book to be both a testimonial to child champions, unique human beings, and a handbook to success.

I will try to share my passion for this sport, for the children, and for the parents who, despite their excesses, are, for the most part, also admirable people.

Learn how to educate a child to become a winner.

Table of contents

Part one

MY JOURNEY/ MY SYSTEM

CHAPTER I
My greatest achievement

1. THE EVENT

January 24, 2006: ten years after I had created my Academy with the purpose of training future tennis champions. The symbol of all those hardworking years surpassed my expectations. Marcos Baghdatis, 20 years old, was playing in the Australian Open semi-final. My Marcos, one of my oldest pupils, whom I welcomed seven years previously, was to face David Nalbandian (3rd seed) that night for a spot in the final of a Grand Slam tournament. Marcos never did things halfway. His first major competition took place during one of the four top tennis meets of the year. My little, 13-year-old kid arrived on top of the world overnight. I reflected back to his arrival in France at such a young age. I was overcome with emotion. His breakthrough was so sudden that it became almost surreal. At the same time, I always knew that this great day would come. I was both stunned and completely impassive when faced with the logic of this scheduled event because everything the entire world was seeing did not really surprise me. Through Marcos' success, I found myself where I had wanted to be since the beginning of my journey. I had done everything necessary to reach this moment. Everything had not always been perfect. I drifted at times or followed the right paths in a blind manner, but I was able to achieve the essential in the end: impart my confidence to others; that elusive magic, that essence of success that achieves great things. Marcos climbed his first Mount Everest that day, and it was a surprise for the entire tennis world. Marcos was certainly

I was able to achieve the essential: impart my confidence to others; that elusive magic, that essence of success that achieves great things.

viewed as a promising player but his world ranking (No.50) and his results would never have foretold such a journey in such a tournament. But Marcos had just eliminated Andy Roddick (No.5) and Ivan Ljubicic (No.4) in Melbourne, which made his presence in the final unquestionable.

2. THE EARLY SIGNS

A surprise? Not to me. I knew Marcos very well and certain signs made me believe that he would "do damage". The telephone call he gave me the week before, following his defeat in the Doha quarter-finals at the hands of the No.1 player in the world, Roger Federer, moved me. His attitude was that of a completely demoralized man. He cried tears of disappointment while any other player would have accepted his defeat as inevitable. Marcos was truly shocked and disappointed with the result. He said: "Pat, if I win the Australian Open, I'll be in the Top 20." He believed it and knew that he was capable. This was an excellent sign.

"Pat, if I win the Australian Open, I'll be in the Top 20.

There he was in the semi-finals ten days later. He had never been closer to winning a Grand Slam title, and, yet he still had a long way to go because he had to win those next two matches. Each one would be a true challenge.

3. MY ARRIVAL

I watched the beginning of the tournament on television. I had remained at the Academy to take care of the younger players and to watch Marcos advance in the rounds. When he won his quarter-final match against Ivan Ljubicic, I decided to go to Melbourne. I jumped into my car and headed for my home to pick up my wife. Our bags were packed in half an hour. In the car, we arranged for babysitting with my in-laws and friends, and headed straight to the airport. We bought two tickets on Singapore Airlines and took off for Australia two hours later. We landed twenty-seven hours later, the morning of the semi-final against the Argentinian, David Nalbandian. I was plagued with memories. A year earlier for his first competition as an adult and ranked No.150, he advanced in the qualification rounds to reach the last sixteen, beating Tommy Robredo (No.15). He called me, absolutely exhilarated, after each match: "Pat, it's amazing! It's absolutely crazy!" But this time he was different; he was calm. He was controlling what was happening to him. He did not have the impression that he was experiencing something incredible. It was great, but it was normal. It was not over. He was very focused, calm, determined and in control of the events.

He is very focused, calm, determined and in control of the events.

When I met up with him, I found that he had changed. It was a very special feeling. His features were different, his expression was not the same as before. His gaze was luminous. Something spectacular lit it up. He had taken on a new dimension, that of a Grand Slam semi-finalist. It was the same Marcos, but not exactly. Amazing!

4. THE MEDIA STORM

This was a huge event for the entire tennis world: the arrival of a new star, bringing a breath of fresh air through a different attitude on the court. Supported by an armada of Greek-Cypriots, who transformed the arena into a soccer stadium, Marcos blew our minds on the court. He was thrilling and communicated his emotions to the public. What more could one ask for? Professional tennis is a show and Marcos is a great "performer". He immediately became a media darling during the tournament and I was greeted in Melbourne by the entire international press.

Upon my arrival, Nicolas Arzani, communications director for the ATP (Association of Tennis Professionals), told me that he had organized a press conference. International sports journalists, won over by the game and personality of the young Cypriot, were hungry for more information about Marcos. I went to the designated meeting place, expecting to find a few specialists. To my great surprise, I found myself in front of four cameras, ten microphones, and a total of twenty journalists from the international print media. The questions rained down. I was not prepared for that type of excitement. That theater of images and sounds where one must tell a story, a real one, was overwhelming, and, yet, I felt comfortable, perfectly at home. I even took pleasure in talking about my passion and about my relationship with Marcos. Many radio stations, television channels and newspapers asked me for interviews following this press conference. They wanted to know all the details of our story...

Professional tennis is a show and Marcos is a great "performer".

5. THE AWAKENING

Game time, 8 pm. I was sitting in the Rod Laver Arena players' box on the center court in Melbourne. There was that mood in the air, right before great moments. The arena was sold-out. Many Greek and Cypriot supporters were present throughout the arena. They were singing, dressed in costume. Some were performing traditional dances in the small, confined spaces of the arena, with their dumbstruck neighbors looking on. There was magic in the air. I felt bizarre before the match began. The day before, I had been overseeing my Academy in Thiverval-Grignon, and suddenly I was in Melbourne, on one of the most mythical of tennis courts.

The day before, I had been overseeing my Academy in Thiverval-Grignon, and suddenly I was in Melbourne, on one of the most mythic of tennis courts.

I awaited the arrival of David Nalbandian and Marcos, **my Marco**s. Caught in the Australian whirlwind those last few hours, during which I had even granted myself the privilege of hitting some shots under the stifling heat, I did not have time to think about what was about to happen. Everything seemed to flow naturally. I suddenly realized the enormity of the situation: this child whom I had seen for the first time in the Petits As tournament in Tarbes when he was only 13 and a half years old; this child whom I had accompanied every morning and every evening from Porte de Champerret to Paris; this child whom I had seen grow up, in height and in confidence, whom I had seen fall in love, happy, sad, with whom I had shared so many things, his triumphs and his defeats, but also his doubts... That was who would arrive in a few moments to the screams of the crowd. The players entered the court, interrupting my thoughts.

I felt like I was watching one of my children perform. Only that the show was being broadcast all over the world, and that only four players in the world were granted the honor of participating...

Back on planet Earth, I felt like I was watching one of my children perform. Only that the show was being broadcast all over the world, and that only four players in the world were granted the honor of participating...

6. THE MATCH

The beginning of the match was one-sided, entirely dominated by Nalbandian. Marcos was tense. He knew that he was playing for a spot in a Grand Slam final. The Argentinian was very confident. He had just won the Masters, beating Roger Federer in the final two months earlier. He was impressive. His down-the-line backhands never ceased, and Marcos, too far from his line, seemed to have trouble keeping up... He quickly found himself trailing two sets to love. He sat in his chair during the end-change. He knew that if he continued on this submissive path, he would return to the locker-rooms very quickly and with huge regrets. Defeat seemed almost inevitable, and yet he refused to surrender. He was ready to fight. He returned to the game newly relaxed and aggressive. He had decided to reconquer the court. And that was exactly what happened. Marcos got near the baseline of the court and took over the game for the first time. The Argentinian, on the other hand, started to stiffen up as he got closer to his first Grand Slam final. Marcos won the third set. He turned to us and with a huge smile, wagged a finger meaning: "It's not over, it's not over!"

The fifth set resembled the fourth. The audience, frenzied before such an incredible scenario and completely won over by Marcos, began chanting his name. The atmosphere was quite simply electric! Nalbandian continued to hold on, unable to accept defeat after getting so close to victory. Five games to four, Baghdatis to serve. Marcos was serving for the match and a spot in a Grand Slam final! And then: a dramatic turn of events! Violent rain poured down onto the court, forcing the organizers to close the retractable roof. The court was drenched, and the players were sent back to the locker-rooms. The wait was unbearable... It is a true test for a player when a match this important is interrupted so close to the end. A player must not lose any upsurge during the break and must be able to return to the court without having had mulled things over during the endless wait so that he can be on top right away. They knew it and Guillaume Peyre, Marcos' coach, also knew it.

"I'm not afraid for you. I'm afraid for him."

When Guillaume entered the locker room to speak with his player, Marcos was petrified.

"I'm afraid, Guillaume."

"I'm not afraid for you. I'm afraid for him."

"..."

"He has everything to lose because he's trailing. He's the favorite and he has the most pressure. Whatever tactics you choose, give 100% of yourself and it will work."

The players were called back onto the court thirty minutes later to finish the match. It was midnight and I had spent twenty-seven hours on a plane; I had a twelve-hour time-lag and had been awake for eighteen hours. I had just received a thirty-five degree thermal shock. I had been in an extraordinarily stressful atmosphere for four hours, and the match was still so indecisive. I have not even mentioned the butterflies in my stomach...

The match resumed. Each point was priceless. I wondered what kind of mental condition they would be in once they returned to the court.

Both players were tense but when Marcos served at his first match point at 40-30, he sent down a magnificent, precise ace. He fell to his knees and cried: "This is huge!" in perfect French, his natural language now.

It was seven minutes past midnight. The crowd was on its feet, and I no longer felt tired since the excitement was at its highest pitch. Yet despite the twists and turns of this unique match, I can honestly say that it was a positive experience. Everything was defined by a continuous search for an ideal. The doubts, the highs, the lows: the match was a metaphor for the bends in our journey: ending up in the spotlight on such a special evening, sitting so close to the players we were almost able to touch them, surrounded by a dizzying din of excitement.

Seven years of hard work were justified by the emotional fireworks the match created. This match gave meaning to everything that had previously been done to get here. I then knew I had taken the right path. And we would take it again and again with the other members of the Academy. Many magical moments awaited us in the future. I had pursued my dream without hesitation and with a belief so strong that my confidence had rebounded onto everyone around me. I had forged ahead without questioning myself. I had not listened

This match gave meaning to everything that had previously been done to get here.

I had forged ahead without questioning myself. I had not listened to the naysayers who argued that my project was too ambitious and unrealistic.

to the naysayers who argued that my project was too ambitious and unrealistic. I had not thought about the negative consequences of possible failure. And ten years after the creation of my Academy, one of my players had reached a Grand Slam final.

7. AN ACCIDENT ?

To better understand what I felt at that moment, we must go back a few years. This moment is particularly joyful because I had worked in the shadows for so many years, up against all of the established powers in the tennis world: the Federation, this multi-millionaire mastodon which has a forty-year monopoly under its belt, and the sports agencies that own many tournaments and are contractually bound to the majority of the great champions. I came across disapproving looks hundreds of times and was subjected to the speeches of French tennis "executives". In the beginning, the entire tennis industry wondered how a highly respected coach like Bob Brett, one of the greatest tennis coaches of this era, could associate his name with mine, a poor Don Quixote with grand, almost indecent, ideas. I had almost no credibility. I knew that, and yet, alone against the powers that be, I firmly held on to what I believed. I knew that I would succeed. Despite the amazing results I had obtained with junior players, my credibility had not improved. And suddenly all the work that I had done over ten years was finally being recognized. The entire tennis world suddenly realized I was there, that I existed and that they had to recognize my work.

I was both happy and frustrated under Melbourne's overpowering heat. The sudden recognition was very nice, but I wanted to tell all of them: "Wake up! My players have reached eight junior Grand Slam finals these past ten years! They won two junior championship titles! Players such as Ancic,

Karlovic and Paul-Henri Mathieu started out with me, and you are just discovering who I am!" One thing is certain: none of these results happened by accident. They were a testament to the quality of work that was carried out.

None of these results happened by accident. They were a testament to the quality of work that was carried out.

Marcos had accomplished a great thing, but the adventure was only just beginning for him. He did not know it yet, but he and I had something in common: we were of the same breed. We had no choice in the matter; we were programmed to win...

We had no choice in the matter; we were programmed to win...

It is difficult to live with that kind of pressure, but it is key when you are working towards accomplishing great things...

I still want more. I am far from satisfied. I want more victories, more emotions. I want to go even further.

I am happy today, but it is only the beginning of the adventure...

CHAPTER 2
My journey

1. MY DREAM – MY QUEST

It took me ten years in the Academy to understand what makes a champion and the principles that must be put in place to train them. It is a subtle chemistry of elements. Training champions has always been the central theme of my life. I was not able to forge an extraordinary career as a professional tennis player, so I wanted to help others do so. It is a constant personal quest. I have asked myself the same questions over the years: "How can I have an impact on a player's future? How can I help them get to the turning points that will make them a great champion? Can they succeed thanks to me and fail elsewhere if given another career path?"

I embarked on this journey with my questions, my passion, my determination and the belief in my ability to find solutions to the problems presented to me.

My initial gamble resided in these terms, and I embarked on this journey with my questions, my passion, my determination and the belief in my ability to find solutions to the problems presented to me. Luckily, all of these questions have been answered today.

The journey I'm on can only make me dream. I share the experiences of exceptional human beings whom I guide with my passion, in accordance with my father's educational principles. He programmed me, willingly or not, according to the founding principles of his way of thinking. In his eyes, a path should not be trodden unless it has a high chance of leading to great success. In other words, my brother and I had no choice but to excel in our respective fields if we wanted to earn his respect.

The cult of perfection was ingrained in me and I was unable to rid myself of it, almost as if it were tattooed onto me, programmed into me. Today no one can convince me that this is not the only way. In other words, I was programmed to win.

The only dark spot in this picture is that my father was not an effective advisor, meaning that he was so focused on his search for personal success, he was only satisfied with imposing the duty of excellence without actually providing the user's manual.

2. HOW MY FATHER RAISED ME

When my father arrived in France from Greece at the age of thirteen, he quickly had to assimilate to his adopted country. He learned the language very quickly and was first in his class by the end of the school year. He earned his high school diploma at seventeen and entered the Ecole Polytechnique the following year. A classical piano virtuoso, he recorded a recital that was recorded and released commercially but he decided to pursue business. Art seemed too risky in his eyes. From that moment on, his thirst for success materialized itself in the form of numerous business projects. Firstly, he built real estate developments in the port of Deauville and Saint Raphaël, and constructed the highest tower in Monaco (Tour de l'Annonciade).

Excellence becomes a burden if one is not accompanied in the endeavor and supported by the trust of an inspirational mentor.

Aside from his exceptional gifts, my father was a relentless and passionate worker. Locked in his world of numbers and classical music, he did not leave room for human relationships. In his opinion, success was a necessity whatever you did. Undertaking a project only had meaning if success was the end result. Bestowing this cult of excellence at all costs can prove to be dangerous however, because excellence becomes a burden if one is not accompanied in the endeavour and supported by the trust of an inspirational mentor.

One must get to the highest levels, but alone. This appears impossible, but either being lousy or great becomes a disturbing perspective insomuch as it is the former that seems the most likely. I avoided the reality of schoolwork because it seemed inaccessible. Left to my own devices in this quest, I just did not feel capable of studying.

I avoided the reality of schoolwork because it seemed inaccessible.

In order to protect my brother and myself from the harsh realities of life, my parents excessively overprotected us. As a child, and then as a young adult disconnected from reality, I was not prepared to face the real world. My parents imparted the values of honesty and excellence without warning me that the world worked in the completely opposite way. When I was attacked at the age of eleven by a boy with a knife who wanted my bike, the shock was incredibly violent for an ignoramus like me.

The positive aspect of this upbringing was that it anchored in me the desire to always do better. It is without a doubt the reason why I wanted to become a champion in my field. But since I felt alone in the face of my responsibilities, it took me a while to incorporate this willpower.

3. ESTRANGED AND LOST

I was scouted by the Hauts de Seine Tennis League at eleven years old. They offered to train me for free since they saw potential in me. I had already been playing tennis with passion, enthusiasm and devotion since the age of six. I just loved the sport! I spent many hours practicing after school and my weekends were played out on a tennis court from morning to night. I beat weary opponents one after the other on a court I never left. I was ranked 30/2 at eleven years old and then I stagnated. However, people who saw me play thought I was doing well. "You have improved technically," they told me. The influence of their confidence in me might have appeared harmless, but it had an immediate effect. I rose to 15/2 like a flash of lightning...

At the age of fifteen, since school hours became incompatible with the daily practice of my sport, I asked my parents to agree upon a special schedule so that I could try my luck as a professional player. But I was only a good player, not an exceptional one. So as for a professional career, the answer was no. It was clear and nonnegotiable. As he had done for himself at the same age, my father preferred security (academia) to risk (art for him, sports for me). My world crumbled.

I knew instinctively that to be an exceptional person in any field, I would have to love it with a folly.

I still have trouble describing exactly what I felt at that moment, and in the hours, the days, the weeks and years that followed. I put tennis behind me for good. I put my rackets away in the closet. They would only come out seven years later. My passion, that which occupied my thoughts, my ambitions, my days and my future, was brutally taken away from me and an immense void was left in its place... But as I often say: "Nature abhors emptiness." I filled this void with years of wandering. I searched for a passion to replace the one that seemed to me so obvious. I knew instinctively that to be an exceptional person in any field, I would have to love it with a folly. I focused on chasing after girls, then music, specifically jazz. I was accepted to the C.I.M (one the best jazz schools in Europe), after showing a certain amount of determination and convinced that I should give my all in every field.

Still adrift, I decided to see a psychologist in order to better understand my troubles and to give meaning to what I loathed to call my life. I therefore took the first steps on this long growth process which lasted ten years.

During those long years, I left home to discover the world my parents had protected me from. If direct contact with reality turned out to be tough, it definitely toughened me up very quickly. I was unoccupied, for I was far from being convinced about my talents, at least for music (chasing after girls does not distinguish you or help you make a living). With my newly acquired high school diploma in my hands, I decided to learn a profession alongside my father. He opened the door of his company for me to do an apprenticeship. I would work by his side for five years, from 20 to 25 years old. My father specialized in the construction of power plants. I entered his company when he diversified into renewable energy. His business was so prosperous that EDF bought a 50% stake in it. His company is quoted on the stock market today.

My life is valuable and I wanted to enhance it by living it fully.

As for me, I was not that thrilled with this introduction to the business world. I learned many interesting things. It was rewarding intellectually but not enough to make me want to make it a life project. At the end of the apprenticeship phase, my father offered me the opportunity to truly work by his side. He wanted to impart his knowledge and teach me how to develop a project from the ground up. He wanted me to become his partner. I was very touched and appreciated the trust he had placed in me, but I refused. "If I look back on my life at the age of 60 and I only see power plants, I won't feel that I have achieved anything. I need to be passionate about it to feel that." My life is valuable and I wanted to enhance it by living it fully. I had to let others experience what I had not had the chance to experience: success at the highest levels of tennis.

My father listened intently and responded: "Very well. I'm disappointed but I understand. As of today, I'll do everything I can to help you achieve your goal."

4. THE CREATION OF THE ACADEMY

I definitively turned the pages of my work experience with my father and decided to dedicate my life to my project.

I did research on all the different training, physical and psychological preparation methods that existed. I obtained the American diploma for tennis instruction, the USPTR, and I founded my Academy T.E.T.C (Tennis Competition Training Team) in the simplest form, with players who were certainly very motivated but who clearly did not have a professional future. This school ran for two years. I was aided by Norbert Palmier, a passionate coach whom I partner with and who works with professional players today. Unfortunately, neither he nor I had the credibility at the time to convince players with potential to join our ranks. I was an illustrious unknown in the tennis world. My competitors were big names. In short, I did not stand a chance... That is when I came up with the idea of getting someone who was credible in the eyes of players to let me use his name and image. At the time, Bob Brett, a 45-year-old Australian coach, was one of the great international references of tennis coaching. He had many Grand Slam victories under his belt and led Boris Becker to the No.1 spot and Goran Ivanisevic to No.2.

It was May 1998. The French Open was approaching and I had to take advantage of the occasion to meet Bob Brett. John Elliot, an Australian who owned a tennis store in Paris, claimed to know him. I asked him to organize a meeting and he did just that for May 27, 1998 at the Warwick Hotel on the Champs-Elysées.

I knew that I only had one hour to convince him. I was very focused. I knew that there would be no second chances.

I knew that I only had one hour to convince him. I was very focused. I knew that there would be no second chances.

We immediately connected and our conversation was interesting:

"What's your goal?" he asked me.

"To work with young players and bring them to the highest international level."

"Why have you come to me? You could have asked Yannick Noah, who is French, for example."

"No. Yannick Noah doesn't interest me. He's a former player, not a coach. He hasn't accomplished what you have. You're the man I need. You have the image and the experience."

After an hour's discussion, he agreed to lend me his name and to be present at the Academy fifty days out of the year, on the condition he be compensated for what he was worth. "I'll return to Paris after Wimbledon. Prepare the contract. We'll sign it then," he told me while giving me a warm handshake.

I was very euphoric after this meeting. I was convinced that I finally had the image I needed to attract many talented players. It was at that moment that my father entered the picture again. I needed significant funds to finance my project in the long term. I did not have any financing and asking my father was the only solution. He kept his promise. He told me: "I believe in your project, so I will finance it." This was a crucial step for me, because I truly needed that money, but also because he implicitly gave me his moral support. I knew how much his judgments were final and without compromise. In showing his faith in my project, he also proved that he had faith in me and thus gave me even more strength to believe in what I was doing.

In showing his faith in my project, he also proved that he had faith in me and thus gave me even more strength to believe in what I was doing.

I met with Bob again after Wimbledon as planned. I had drafted the contract in French. Bob wanted it to be translated into English, but I explained to him: "We don't have time, Bob. I don't have any players, coaches, or an infrastructure to set up the Academy. It's early July and everything must be ready by September. If I have to get the contract translated, I won't see you again for another few weeks and we won't be ready in time." He therefore trusted me and signed the French contract without understanding a word.

My idea: to create a small group of hand-picked players with great potential and to customize their training, whereas every other academy only focuses on volume.

That is how TETC Bob Brett was born.

My idea: to create a small group of hand-picked players with great potential and to customize their training, whereas every other academy only focused on volume.

That was my initial idea and it has remained one of the guiding principles of my entire work.

5. THE EARLY DAYS OF TETC BOB BRETT

Thanks to Bob's support, I took meetings with many agents so that they could help me get started by advising their players to train with me. My pitch stayed true to my principles: "Trust me. I have the best coach in the world at my side. I have the financing for the project and the motivation. I will succeed. In a few years, my Academy will be a leading player in the tennis world and many of the best players will train here. If you help me get started by suggesting our services to your rising players, I guarantee to do everything I can to make sure that my players will sign with you in the future."

I particularly remember a discussion at the Octagon headquarters with the director of the French division, Jorge Salkeld, and his main agent, Laurent Rizzo.

"We won't do anything for the moment, Patrick. Prove yourself and then we'll see."

"I need your help now. Your help will no longer be useful once I've proven myself."

"We won't do anything until you've proven yourself."

"That's too bad. You could have had an ally. You'll now have an additional competitor, because if you don't help me, then I'll manage the players myself."

"Do you think it's easy? It's a profession you know nothing about. You won't be able to do it."

"Oh, really? Do you see Laurent who's sitting next to you? Well, if I decide to go into sports management, I'll partner with him."

I didn't know this Laurent, but their reaction frustrated me. I found it annoying and stupid. In 1999, I decided to create my own sports management agency. I convinced Laurent Rizzo from Octagon to partner with me. Jorge Salkeld called me right away on my mobile phone: "You can't do this! I've been training him for three years!"

"Sorry Jorge, but that's not my problem. We've reached an agreement, and from now on you have one more competitor!"

It was the beginning of a partnership that would last six years, during which we lived every day with the feeling that we were alone, fighting with our meager means. I often thought about the early days of Microsoft or Apple, of these students who invented products in the darkness of their garages. With Laurent, we shared many emotions, laughs and friendship.

I often thought about the early days of Microsoft or Apple, of these students who invented products in the darkness of their garages.

There I was, parachuted into the world of professional tennis overnight, into this small microcosm where everyone knows each other, watches each other, sizes each other up. And me, I was a complete unknown.

It was not long before everyone put their two cents in, especially the equipment suppliers, coaches and Bob's friends who questioned his choice: "How can you associate your name to the project of a man no one knows? It is completely irresponsible." Yet Bob believed in me and my project. He supported me. "You haven't heard of him, but he's very good and I'm certain that his project will lead to something. He has everything: financing, ambition, energy, determination and work. You'll see what he's capable of."

On my end, I sold Bob Brett wherever I could. I organized a big open-house with Bob present in order to convince a few tennis hopefuls to join us. I did not have any hang-ups and I did not bother myself with unnecessary questions. My marketing angle was simple: "The master is in Paris!" Alexandre Sidorenko and Irena Pavlovic, two 10-year-old players from Eastern Europe, were the first whose parents believed in my project. It was then that I finally opened the doors to my Academy, located in Montreuil, in September 1998.

I did not have any hang-ups and I did not bother myself with unnecessary questions.

The day after the opening, someone from the Paris League came to the Academy: the first of many surprises. It should be noted that at that time the French Tennis Federation, with its network of leagues all over the country, was an institution. No competitor had survived their dominance.

"You're Mouratoglou?"

"Yes."

"There's a problem. You're on our territory. (deux espaces!)"

"That's too bad because I'm here to stay."

"You have to go see the president of the League. He wants to know what you're up to."

I obeyed. He tried to make me understand that the FFT trained the best players and that that would not change. However, if the "second and third stringers" (I found this term to be very elegant, especially concerning players who, once having become "first stringers", were courted by everyone) interested me, I could always train them.

I began my project in this extremely tense environment. But it takes more to discourage me. I have a profusion of energy and enthusiasm. I take a hit, I give two back. So I revealed to the press my thoughts on the FFT's immobilization, and it created a few waves in the profession. In hindsight, my actions were futile. I bothered them, so they tried to discourage me. On my end, I should not have gotten into a boxing match with them. It was not productive... It would have been better to just concentrate on the most important thing: making my project a success. It was an error of youth, but I was too enthusiastic and thought I was indestructible.

I bothered them, so they tried to discourage me. On my end, I should not have gotten into a boxing match with them.

I decided to scout the Tarbes tournament to recruit foreign players. I was searching for the rare gem and Marcos Baghdatis was the first to catch my eye. He was not exactly the best, and actually no one noticed him. But he was different from the others in his way of doing things. He stood straight, made a sign of the cross when he stepped onto the court. He was charismatic and hit the ball hard. It was love at first sight.

Paradoxically, I had an advantage over other people in the profession: I knew nothing. As a result, I arrived on the scene without the experience or preconceived ideas that too often prevent others from advancing.

Paradoxically, I had an advantage over other people in the profession: I knew nothing. As a result, I arrived on the scene without the experience or preconceived ideas that too often prevent others from advancing.

I read anything I could get my hands on. I devoured every book on tennis, instruction, coaching, personal development, and tried to draw anything from this pool of knowledge that can be applicable to tennis. I particularly liked Anthony Robbins (the American author of "Unlimited Power", a bestseller) whose positive energy touched me, and I tried to find a way to apply some of his methods to tennis coaching. I was a sponge. I had no hang-ups and sought advice from anyone likely to help me flesh out my ideas.

I gathered my staff every morning to give the momentum and energy for the day.

Bob Brett helped me a lot. He insisted that I come to the court with him as much as possible. He showed me his "stuff", made me participate and explained things to me. He prepared

Bob Brett showed me his "stuff", made me participate and explained things to me. He prepared and trained me.

and trained me. I sensed in him a desire, a joy of transferring his knowledge that was rich from twenty years of experience on the professional circuit and with so many great victories under his belt! Bob was by far the coach who most inspired me on many levels. Things started to gradually take shape in my mind.

6. MOURATOGLOU "TENNIS ACADEMY"

My relationship with Bob Brett started to deteriorate in 2003. Our relationship was almost filial, and he could not accept the fact that I was seeking advice from other people. It hurt him that he was not my only source of information and he viewed it as infidelity on my part. He addressed me in terms that still resound in my head today because they so surprised and shocked me: "You betrayed me. It's like a relationship with a woman. The relationship is over once one of them cheats." This seemed a bit excessive to me. I admit to having certain faults, but I place the blame more on passion and enthusiasm than a lack of respect or commitment.

The support from the players and their parents warmed my heart, and my motivation to continue the journey was strengthened.

From that moment on, our relationship was very tense and it dawned on me that I had invested everything in Bob Brett's name and image. If he decided to leave, it would be extremely harmful to me. After much thought, I decided to end our partnership. Later on, I discovered that he had founded another Academy in Italy months earlier, and that he had asked players from my Academy to join him.

I was so disgusted that I was ready to abandon everything. The players persuaded me to continue:

"We are with you... you have to continue." I particularly remember the words of Marcos' father, whose son had just been crowned world junior champion. "If you need to, use Marcos' image as much as you want to promote the Academy, but you cannot give up! The players need you." The support from the players and their parents warmed my heart, and my motivation to continue the journey was strengthened.

But I had to rethink everything. I decided to keep the Academy's original name, "TETC", for a while. Then, I attended a junior tournament, the O.U.A.T.T. (Once Upon a Time Tennis), a kind of world championship where the players competed by year of birth. This event was organized by a friend and associate, Philippe Sautet, an extremely enthusiastic and creative person. During the evening events, in front of the players and their parents, he handed me a microphone to promote my Academy. Afterwards, many parents came up to me and asked me to evaluate their children's skills, which I did happily. The following day, during a dinner with Philippe Sautet, he tried to convince me: "Give your Academy your name. Every Academy in the world carries the name of its founder. You've done the work from the beginning. Don't have any hang-ups."

That is how TETC Bob Brett became MOURATOGLOU Tennis Academy.

7. MY RESULTS

We have come a long way since 1998, and the Academy already has a great history behind it: two world junior championship titles with Gilles Muller, the Luxembourg player, in 2001, then with Marcos Baghdatis in 2003. The latter is still at the Academy eight years after his arrival, and has been in the international Top 10. The former left us a year after his championship title. He was ranked No.200 in the ATP rankings at the time.

Academy players have reached eight junior Grand Slam finals, won an Orange Bowl and played in a Petits As final in Tarbes.

Many talented players were trained or have worked at the Academy for one or two years. This is the case for Nicolas Kiefer,

Hicham Arazi (finalist in the Masters Series in Monte Carlo while he trained at the Academy), Paul-Henri Mathieu (winner of the French Open Junior Championship, while he trained at the Academy), Mario Ancic (Australian Open and Wimbledon junior finalist), Ivo Karlovic, Nicolas Coutelot, Dick Norman, and many others...

Two world junior championship titles. Eight junior Grand Slam finals and numerous titles...

Today, in addition to the young players who are the best in the world within their age category, the 2006 junior world champion, Anastasia Pavlyuchenkova, and the number three junior player, Ksenia Milevskaya, train at Thiverval, just like Marcos Baghdatis and Julia Vakulenko (No.33 in the world as of January 15, 2007).

CHAPTER 3
At my place in Thiverval

1. WHAT IS SUCCESS?

After Marcos Baghdatis' Australian Open final, one of my friends sent me a text message: "All the people who took you for a crazy man are now going to think you are a genius!" That is the magic of the tennis world. People judge you by your results.

In professional tennis, anything you do is considered worthless if you do not produce results. It is our reason for existing and our legitimacy.

Anything you do is considered worthless if you do not produce results. But when the results are there, you become credible. It is the law of the profession and I accept it. Even more, I approve of it and swear by it. An idea is not worthy in the professional world if it does not produce results. It is our reason for existing and our legitimacy.

When I arrived in the professional tennis world with innovative ideas ten years ago, people thought I was crazy, an idealist and a dreamer. But that did not stop me. Convinced of the validity of my method, I persevered until the day I would be able to prove the effects. I knew that this day would come. I knew that one day I would get to the top of my profession because I knew my potential and how determined I was. I had a plan and I would bring it to fruition.

I knew that one day I would get to the top of my profession because I knew my potential and how determined I was.

2. CUSTOMIZATION VERSUS VOLUME

My main idea consisted of offering customized training to the players I selected to enter my Academy. While other training centers or academies proposed a system founded on natural selection by shuffling a high volume of players, I promised individual preparation to each one of my unique protégés. Completely different to other academies I had come across.

I dreamt of turning pro when I was eleven years old, and wanted to know everything about tennis. It was at that time that I heard about tennis academies for the first time. The first to make a name for itself was the Nick Bollettieri Academy. It made you dream. Long articles in specialized newspapers at the time described the ins and outs of this system of natural selection. Everyone has access to it; it is just a question of price. In reality, it is no more and no less than a tennis version of the American dream. The Nick Bollettieri Academy is essentially made up of rising players and parents who dream of fame. Anything is possible. Each player fights to have the best coaches, the best physical trainers... and each one tries his luck in the great adventure that is professional tennis.

Although French tennis magazines tried to remain objective by also showing what happened behind the scenes, it was not enough to discourage my childhood dream. Thanks to its results, the Bollettieri system has gained an enormous following and serves as a model for generations of professional players all over the world.

When I started out, everyone agreed that reaching a professional level was uncertain. That is why the only worthy system is natural selection. It is important to have the largest number of players and to train them all. One or two will stand out in the end. I do not like that type of reasoning. I am sure we can do better than that. I also think that we can propose a project that is more respectful of human beings.

My idea is contrary to the idea of mass training: if I can understand what gets a player to the top of the international hierarchy, I can select the players according to my standards. If they have the potential, and I am able to identify their needs, I can deliver customization and make them champions. I view them as Formula 1 racing cars that you constantly have to fine-tune in order to reach peak potential, whereas in someone else's hands they would be treated as a common car. What a project! That was the concept that I presented to the main actors in the tennis world in 1998, supported by Bob Brett. And I also got criticized for it.

I view them as Formula 1 racing cars that you constantly have to fine-tune in order to reach peak potential, whereas in someone else's hands they would be treated as a common car.

Yet, my model is copied today. Many Federations have decided to reduce the number of players they take on and to improve the quality of their services. In short, they have decided to be closer to their players.

3. MY SYSTEM

My dynamic is different from the Bollettieri method. I invest my own money and energy into these players, thus proving my good faith. It is too easy to say that this player or that player will go far. Yet, everyone does just that in tennis. On the other hand, investing on a human level and financially in a young player is another story, a story of convictions, a story of people.

Only when Academy players succeed do they pay me back, out of their winnings from pro tournaments. I take risks. But I have faith! Thanks to the funds my father invested in my venture, I was able to launch the operation and protect myself mid-term while waiting for the first fruits of my success. By deciding to invest myself 100% into players, I was able to gradually develop the method I apply when training my own coaches. Disappointed by the results of independent coaches, I decided to train my entire team myself. Today, the Mouratoglou Academy is located in Thiverval, within a basin in the Yvelines countryside, a few kilometers from Paris. Bordering the courts, which run the gamut of surfaces used on the circuit, about a dozen lodges, named "Chalets", are spacious enough to house an entire family if necessary.

Only when Academy players succeed do they pay me back, out of their winnings from pro tournaments. I take risks. But I have faith!

4. MY PHYSICAL AND MEDICAL TEAM

My Academy epitomizes the cult of performance, therefore professionalism. Throughout the years, I have selected a small group of highly skilled professionals in their respective fields: from physical preparation to psychology, to osteopathy, physical therapy, traumatology and nutrition, I work with the best. I believe that we must all be very professional. We are responsible and we must assume our responsibilities. It is therefore necessary to be surrounded by the best. Throughout this ten year trek, I have met many specialists; some good, some bad, some geniuses, and some crazy ones...

I have a very touching memory of a physical therapist who was part of my team for five years and who left a lasting mark on me. His name is Roger Le Guennec and he has unfortunately passed away. His passion, his intelligence, his perceptive eye and his capacity to analyze made him an unforgettable person. He was ahead of his time and suffered for it. He became a friend, and I wanted to write a few words so that he would know that I have not forgotten about him.

Physical preparation is essential to athletic performance for many reasons: when it is well-controlled, it constitutes the best barrier against injury.

Physical preparation is essential to athletic performance for many reasons: when it is well-controlled, it constitutes the best barrier against injury. It also directly affects self-confidence. And finally, it often makes the difference in modern sports which are dominated by professionals.

In 2000, I met a man who is still with me today. His name is Christophe Hausswirth, and he works as a researcher at INSEP (National Institute of Sports and Physical Education). Christophe was a professional triathlete when we first met. He is one of the ten best European triathletes and trains three times a day! Despite his overloaded schedule, he found the time to obtain his doctorate in physiology, become a researcher at INSEP, and a physical trainer. Since 2000, together we offer a carefully thought out, supervised and scientifically controlled physical preparation program. A major first in tennis!

And we are going even further today. Christophe is also a nutritionist. He monitors the players' diets and verifies the proper functioning of their bodies throughout the year. He has even found the time to create an energy drink which is sold in pharmacies and the effects of which on performance and the quality of recuperation have been scientifically proven: Isoxan Sport Pro.

Physical training directly affects self-confidence.

Christophe works at the Academy in collaboration with a tennis physical training specialist: Sébastien Durand. Seb is another extraordinary man whom I am lucky to have at my side. He is also a tennis coach, which allows him to perfectly understand the activity itself. He is a sports fanatic, an extremely hard worker and has an irresistible, contagious enthusiasm. He is very charismatic, highly creative, and yet he challenges himself every day. To top it all off, he is a very good listener. In short, he is a great coach. Today, Seb has three very promising assistants who follow his steps with much enthusiasm.

To be truly effective, physical training must work in close collaboration with the physical therapist and osteopath because all three work on the same instrument, the human body. Each discipline brings a complementary vision that allows a better understanding of the whole.

I was lucky to have met an exceptional osteopath. It took a while to find the right person and I had numerous disappointing experiences. I am pragmatic. I want results! On the advice of a player, I ended up meeting François Teissedre D'Alou, who talked to me about his profession. François has a diploma in physical therapy and training, but also has a French and English osteopathy diploma. He works in the latter field. His explanations and professional resumé were captivating, but I had no idea what kind of results he could obtain. At that time, three of my Academy players had medical setbacks: one had had a groin injury for three months; another had had periodic periostitis for two years; and the third had had a pain in his thumb for four months, an injury which prevented him from holding his racket correctly. Every treatment had failed and these stubborn ills kept my players off the court.

With François, jokes fly and energy overflows! Everything goes very quickly; it is like being in a tornado. At the end of the session, the pain goes away and the player is as good as new.

I therefore asked François to meet them and offer solutions. In all three cases, the medical problems were resolved two weeks following the consultation. The periostitis case was the most impressive; it was completely gone in one session. The player got up and François told her: "It's over. You'll no longer be in pain. You can start playing again." She has never had a case of periostitis since that day! In terms of effectiveness, I did not need any more convincing. I also like his rational approach to problems. François explains things. I know that there is no magic involved, just a mechanical mastery that treats and cures.

François is a unique person. Every session is a performance, a show. Jokes fly and energy overflows! Everything goes very quickly; it is like being in a tornado. At the end of the session, the pain goes away and the player is as good as new.

5. MY TENNIS TEAM

There is no school to become a coach, no training. The majority of coaches on the tennis circuit are self-made men.

There is no school to become a coach, no training. The majority of coaches on the tennis circuit are self-made men. I trusted "experienced" coaches during my early years in the profession and was constantly disappointed by their mediocre results. At the same time, I was slowly creating my own method, and I decided to test it out on young coaches who fit the profile and had the potential to become aces. I am presently assisted by an athletic director, Jean-Paul Damit, who was Marcos Baghdatis' former coach and who has become my friend. He understands me perfectly and knows my method by heart. Therefore he is naturally the ideal person to support, encourage and improve my coaching team every day. He is charismatic and full of energy, and moreover, I have complete trust in him.

One of the greatest difficulties in this profession is having a point of view and positive attitude in an environment that does not necessarily lend itself to that.

The day I understood what was truly needed to succeed, I relentlessly fought against my penchant for negative thinking. I continue to force myself to have a positive mentality every day. We must preserve this mentality in everything we do, including when we make mistakes, because it is the lessons we learn from those mistakes that allow us to grow. That is the dilemma in our profession. How can one be completely involved and perfectly detached at the same time? When you are in a bubble with a player, emotions often gain the upper hand and it becomes difficult to keep a positive attitude. A player's parent who breaks a racket out of scorn during a match will find it hard to remain calm and will be consumed by negativity. It is important to distance oneself in this kind of situation and take a break to reflect on it. If the player has experienced a setback, instead of getting angry, one must take the time ask oneself: "Here is the situation. How can I help him? What words should I use to help him overcome his difficulty and find a solution?" I have learned to keep my calm in any situation. I have certainly made mistakes with my words and actions, but I never make a comment to a player without having had thought it out first.

How can one be completely involved and perfectly detached at the same time? When you are in a bubble with a player, emotions often gain the upper hand and it becomes difficult to keep a positive attitude.

Following this principle, Jean-Paul Damit trains coaches to reason and to think the right way. He teaches them to communicate with the right words, to give their players confidence in themselves. He chooses coaches who still have this ability to listen and are open-minded, and who are not against questioning their methods. If they show the necessary potential, they will make very good coaches. I am especially

He chooses coaches who still have this ability to listen and are open-minded, and who are not against questioning their methods.

proud of Guillaume Peyre, who arrived at the Academy at a young age, and who, after having accompanied Marcos to No.8 in the world , is now recognized as one of the best coaches on the circuit. Jean-Paul's and my objective is to allow others to reach that level.

6. THE FAMILY AS THE CEMENT FOR SUCCESS

One of the important requirements for success is to have someone by your side who believes in your abilities as a player.

One of the important requirements for success is to have someone by your side who believes in your abilities as a player.

Do not think that I am stating the obvious. It is impossible to succeed without this basic idea, even if you possess a strong, fearless soul or had the best education. The tennis world is too risky to succeed alone. Moments of doubt can be swept aside with the flick of a hand if a player has a good support system and if the right words are spoken at the right moment. On the other hand, if a player does not have this support system, or if his entourage does not truly believe in him, the slightest hint of doubt immediately becomes a crisis of confidence. The player thus enters the vicious cycle of defeat. The vast majority of champions are made up of men and women who are able to maintain a stable entourage. This entourage remains faithful to the player because they understand how important it is to do so. Good players sometimes change coaches. Very good players rarely do so. Björn Borg remained with Lennart Bergelin his entire career. Sampras and Roger Federer also live in an unchanging environment. André Agassi had long term relationships with all of his trainers.

Another shining example, Jim Courrier, the "unbeatable" No.1 champion, fell to twentieth place almost overnight after he separated from his longtime coach. However much he fought, he was never able to reach the Top 10 again. I have seen players fall into obscurity and make a huge comeback thanks to people who showed them that they truly believed in them. I have seen players break down because their entourage walked out on them. Self-confidence, which is greatly influenced by how other people view you, is key. Self-confidence determines if a match is won or lost... the confidence that others give you has a very particular flavor and value...

The family is the first to believe in their child's ability to become a great athlete. The majority of great tennis success stories begin with a family plan. Knowing this, I made the decision early on to work with parents. Other institutions reject them, arguing that they know nothing about tennis. On the contrary, I think that they are the essence and the cement for success. Everything is more complicated without them and the chances for success diminish all the more. They are, of course, far from perfect; but then again who is? And how would we react if it were our own children? Ask ourselves these questions and we will be less critical of them.

The vast majority of champions are made up of men and women who are able to maintain a stable entourage. This entourage remains faithful to the player because they understand how important it is to do so.

I have always viewed parents as my partners. We have many things in common and we have the same goal. Add to that respect, mutual understanding, solid teamwork, and success is inevitably at hand. I prefer to work with parents on the court for these reasons. I try to teach them my method to make their child a champion, and they give me the keys I need to better communicate with them.

Together, we build the self-confidence of the young player thanks to this union.

Part two
MY METHOD

Introduction: Various questions

"If you give a man a fish, he will eat for a day. If you teach him how to fish, he will always have food to eat."
(Chinese proverb)

Ask parents what they want for their children and the answer to this question greatly depends on each person's culture and way of thinking. In our Western democracies, it is summed up in one sentence: "I want my children to be happy." What an agenda...

There is not a universal definition of happiness. Happiness is subjective, and parents set a paradoxically subjective and extremely vague goal for their children.

Happy, yes, but how? What is happiness? Will what makes me happy make you happy? So many questions, the answers to which are vague to say the least. The problem is simple: there is not a universal definition. Happiness is subjective, meaning that parents set a paradoxically subjective and extremely vague goal for their children. There is no need to point out that the chances for success are doubtful and that the educational methods are not very structured.

My alternative is to teach children to set goals and to give them the means to achieve those goals. In this way, when they reach adulthood they will decide what to make of their lives. Imagine that your son has decided to become a car racer. He can do it. Anything is possible.

Most people do not set goals, mainly because they do not believe that they have the ability to achieve them. Would you say that they are happy? No, probably not. On the other hand, you probably know a few lucky people who have ambitions and dreams.

That is how I would define happiness: that capacity to dream and to make those dreams a reality! Every dream that is achieved must leave room for a new ambition. At least that is what I hope for my own children.

A champion is someone who is able to set important goals and reach them.

People who are able to accomplish their dreams are "great people", and those who reach their most lofty goals are champions. Every child can be exceptional if they develop the capacity to set their goals and to obtain what they expect from life.

In my opinion, every child can become a champion. It only depends on their parents and their support system.

A child is a clean slate at birth, and his or her potential in any activity, be it intellectual, physical or artistic, is unlimited. In the first years of his or her life, based on their observations and by interpreting them according to their beliefs, parents form a very precise opinion of their child: he or she has this skill, this flaw; he or she is gifted in this but terrible in that. Thus they unconsciously and unintentionally indicate to the child how to grow up, in which activity, with what skills, and which faults to watch out for. In general, the more confidence and positive attitude the parents have, the more the child will perceive encouragement, and therefore, will have fewer limited beliefs. However, people lacking in self-confidence pass on their doubts in the form of limits to their children, because it is much more reassuring to believe that something is unnachievable when we feel that we are unable to do it.

Every child has unlimited potential... up until the moment their parents put limits on their development.

I would add that this applies to any activity. "Great parents" have shown us the way, notably in professional tennis, since parents like Richard Williams (father of Venus and Serena) or Earl Woods (father of Tiger Woods), to name but a few, have enabled their children to become great champions while they were only novices in the subject matter.

Physical aptitudes do not make a sports champion; personality and a strong mind do.

That is why, for almost ten years now, I have not agreed with the theories of coaches or of certain Federations. I am convinced that the essence is not found in the sport but in the mental qualities of the athletes. Mental qualities are acquired at a very young age and directly depend on the education a child's parents have given them.

We knowingly or unconsciously brand our children with a red iron for their entire life. We instill values in them, a degree of confidence in themselves, and beliefs. Their relationships with others and their future as adults are determined at a very early age. We program our children even if we refuse to accept that fact.

In this book, I outline my method for turning your children into champions.

HOW IS A CHAMPION MADE?

Almost all champions are primarily the product of their parents' crazy dream. Must we mention Agassi, Seles, Graf, the Williams sisters, Hingis, Sharapova and Djokovic to be convinced?

Parents one day decide to launch themselves in an absolutely crazy adventure. They do not have a method, just a project, hope, determination and perseverance. The risk of eventual failure is great. Failure would have grave, even irreversible, repercussions. Yet each year and in every field, whether it is art, sports or academia, parents decide to make their children into champions.

Champions are born from the decision parents make to launch themselves in a completely crazy adventure.

Children need a rigid framework. They need goals. If we consider that the role of the educator consists of teaching children to become capable, successful adults, then we must prepare them at a very young age to establish goals and to work towards their fruition.

Nothing is more reassuring for children than knowing exactly what their parents expect of them.

Young children find it difficult to set their own goals simply because they lack experience. That is why parents must do it for them. Then parents and children can work together, sometimes with the help of professionals, to achieve a project. Take the case of the young Jan Silva, an American child who arrived at the Academy with his parents at the age of four. His parents decided to surround themselves with professionals in order to carry through their project. At the same time, the reason this young child has developed such impressive skills, it is mainly because his parents never set limits for him for they are convinced that he has unlimited potential. The goal is clear and the means of achieving it are even clearer. Every day is another step towards success. Parents must have a goal and a battle plan. Tennis is just one example; it is not better or worse than another. You must know that the accomplishment of the project will take time and that you must be patient.

Nothing is more reassuring for children than knowing exactly what their parents expect of them. There is nothing better than to wake up in the morning knowing what they must do that day; there is nothing more motivating than having a goal, an objective to work towards every day.

CAN MY CHILD BECOME A CHAMPION?

Yes, he can. It is a question of method, determination, and discipline.

Parents who have applied a rigorous, workable method have allowed their children to accomplish great things.

Parents who have applied a rigorous, workable method have allowed their children to accomplish great things. Venus and Serena Williams' father is a shining example. He decided at their birth that they would become tennis champions and they both went on to reach the heights of the world rankings. His method: the one I will outline for you in the following pages. Richard Williams does not leave anything to chance. He is methodical, rigorous and exemplary. Tiger Woods' father also used the same method, as did André Agassi's parents. It is also the reason why the young Jan Silva shows such aptitudes. He was educated to win even before he could walk.

Contrary to an idea firmly ingrained in the minds of the general public, success is not a question of talent. Of course, we are not all born equal. Some people have exceptional abilities, but those abilities do not make them champions.

A champion is above all a personality, an exceptional person, a very unique nature and psychology. Athletics is a form of expression, like art. True sensibility can express itself once the tools have been mastered. That is the difference between a simple musician, a talented musician and a prodigy. It is also what differentiates a Top 200 tennis player from a Top 50 player and a Grand Slam winner.

That is the difference between a genius and a simple musician, and a great champion and a very good tennis player. It depends on the personality of the player.

To prove my point, observe the games of Lleyton Hewitt, Andy Roddick, Rafael Nadal, Maria Sharapova and Venus Williams. These players have one thing in common: the personality of a champion. Their talent is not immense, maybe even inferior to many talented players who do not have their track record, but their self-confidence, their fighting spirit, and their strength of character are unique.

All of these traits are the results of education; the education their parents gave them. Every child has the ability to become a champion, and each one of us has the potential to give them this opportunity.

Every child has the ability to become a champion, and each one of us has the potential to give them this opportunity.

WHAT IF MY CHILD IS NOT GIFTED?

It is impossible to answer this question before you have given him a chance, before you have taught him how to work and

We cannot conclude that a child is gifted or not in a sport before having tried it and without believing that he will succeed.

fight, before you have developed his motor skills, and before you have introduced him to the activity.

He will surprise you with his skills on the court. Every child has great potential, but in the majority of cases, it is abandoned by parents who doubt his abilities.

Tennis is one of the richest and most complex sports that exist. The required qualities to become a great player are vast, and one can easily be replaced by another. If your child is not physically strong, he will have hand skills, tactical skills, mental skills or technical skills... And as we have seen before, the key is that the child must possess the mind of a champion.

But how can you make that happen?

DOES THE PRESSURE CREATED BY THE DAILY PRACTICE OF A SPORT PUT IN DANGER MY CHILD'S PSYCHOLOGICAL WELL-BEING OR PHYSICAL HEALTH?

A 6-year-old child possesses an unlimited amount of energy. What they accomplish on a physical level is worthy of the best adult athletes.

Have you already spent an entire day with a 6-year-old? If so, you have probably noticed the exceeding amount of energy they burn. You have most certainly noticed their immense ability to listen, imitate, concentrate and learn when they are interested in something.

This period in a child's life is exceptional because the child is busy growing. Nature being well made, it gives us the tools to accomplish the mission entrusted to us: to build our future.

They should channel a part of their enormous energy in a constructive activity.

You just have to observe a 6-year-old playing all day with friends of the same age. What they accomplish on a physical level is worthy of the best adult athletes. The child knows this innately because he possesses boundless energy in the face of any challenge.

A few years ago, a very interesting experiment was performed: professional athletes were hired to physically reenact the typical day of a 6-year-old. This turned out to be too difficult for them to handle on a resistance level.

I am not advocating that children be overly trained, but they should channel a part of their enormous energy in a constructive activity. It is also an opportunity to teach them how to use this energy instead of scattering it. They should be introduced to a range of activities in order to offer them one or more goals. A child needs a framework within which to grow. Traditional school is one. It promotes the development of the mind. It offers a structure that allows the child to enrich himself and to prepare for the future. But traditional school hardly bothers with the development of the child's body. Yet the body, just like the mind, needs a framework within which to blossom.

The body and the mind both need to be developed.

Human beings have lived under pressure for thousands of years. The pressure to find the necessary food for survival, to fight to stay alive, and today, to find work in a difficult environment, to enter society...

A parent's role is to prepare his child to be ready to face the real world that awaits him. That is actually what school offers with its system of grades, so that, at a very young age, children can get used to meeting standards and to obtaining results.

Pressure is inherent to our nature as human beings, and the story of Man is about the fight to survive. What pressure!

IS THE IDEA OF "PROGRAMMING" MY CHILD ACCEPTABLE ON AN ETHICAL LEVEL?

The term, programming, has an extremely negative connotation. It implies that the child does not have free will, but reproduces protocols the parents have ingrained in him at an early age.

Psychoanalysis has helped us understand to what extent our education and our childhood experiences influence our minds.

Without going to such extremes, the discovery and the development of psychoanalysis has helped us understand to what extent our education and our childhood experiences influence our psychology, so much so that they unconsciously guide us in the choices we make as adults.

These ideas, while built into our modern culture, remain difficult to accept.

Yet, if the term "programming" seems aggressive, we must accept the idea that we leave an imprint on the psychology of our children which will greatly determine the quality of their future.

Just like the 19th-century baker who passes on his love for his profession to his children, the modern parent gives them a view of life that irreversibly influences the future adults they will become.

Just like the 19th-century baker who imparts his love for his profession and his knowledge to his children, the modern parent gives them a view of life and of their own self-perception. All of these parameters irreversibly influence the future adult he is raising each day.

In other words, parents unintentionally program their children. They are not completely aware of the consequences of their acts and do not always have a clear project. It is therefore a kind of natural selection that occurs as a result. If we want our children to be happy in the future, they must have the tools to obtain what they want from life. The foundation of their psychology must be oriented towards performance for this to happen.

AND WHAT IF HE DOES NOT LIKE TENNIS (OR THE ACTIVITY I HAVE CHOSEN FOR HIM)?

The notion of liking an activity is closely linked to the feeling of success that comes with it.

Your children will like tennis if you like it. Your children will like tennis if you love them, if you have a close relationship with them, if you allow them to share your love for the game. They will love tennis if you present it as a game; they will love tennis if you "play" with them. If they can associate positive and empowering experiences with it, then they will want to play it.

Have confidence in yourself, and you will be able to share your passions with your children.

The notion of liking an activity is closely linked to the feeling of success that comes with it.

Here is an example. One day, your mother teaches you how to make a difficult dish. The next day you make it for your family and everyone loves it. They swoon over it and you receive wonderful compliments. Even better, your brother, your sister and your parents cannot stop praising your talents: "You are a gifted cook! What talent! Thank you so much, it was delicious!" Inspired by this first success and having learnt that your parents have invited guests to dinner the following week, you offer to make the dish again. You receive the same warm reception, which pushes you to try new recipes. You quickly become the appointed family cook.

You improve little by little, and gradually, you discover and then master the subtleties of this field.

You love to cook because it makes you worthy in the eyes of others and in turn gives you personal satisfaction. That is how you persevere and try to improve constantly. Your interest in cooking grows with each new success and you end up becoming so passionate about it that you perfectly master the subject.

Any kind of activity can be interesting; the teacher makes all the difference.

In conclusion, if you want your child to be interested in an activity, you must be able to adequately teach it to them. Any kind of activity can be interesting; the teacher makes all the difference.

AND WHAT IF MY CHILD CANNOT DO IT?

This is probably the most common remark I have heard. It is unfortunately the most "French". Why is that, in this country, failure is systematically the first possible hypothesis any time someone wants to start a project?

Failure is a state of mind. It only exists for those who conceive of it.

The very idea of failure is terrifying and never causes you to act. To envision failure is to give yourself every reason in the world not to try. It prepares you to abandon ship when the slightest difficulty arises. No, the only way to succeed is to dive right into your project.

As Dan Millman writes in "Way of the Peaceful Warrior" when talking about moderation: "It is better to make a mistake with every power in your being than to carefully avoid mistakes with a trembling heart. Being responsible means knowing pleasure as well as its price, making a choice based on this knowledge, and then living this choice without any anxiety... [...]

Moderation? Moderation is mediocrity, fear and confusion disguised [...] Compromise does not satisfy anyone. Moderation is for weak and scared people, for those who are unable to take a stand. It is for those who are afraid to laugh or to cry, for those who are afraid of living or dying."

To envision failure means that you are not committed.

It takes commitment to succeed in your life or in your children's. Commitment is the enemy of moderation and fear. To envision failure means that you are not committed.

Would they have taken such risks if they had given one thought to failure?

Did Jan Silva's parents hesitate? Did they think of failure when they made the decision to radically change their lives in order to give their 4-year-old son the best chance at success?

Scott and Mari are amazing people. They abandoned their American life, their friends, the climate, to move to my Academy in Thiverval-Grignon. They quit their jobs. They sold their house. They took every risk in order to offer their child the best. Would they have done so if they had given one thought to failure? Now think as to why Jan is so strong, so talented, so sure of himself, so radiant at such a young age. His parents show him all the force of their belief in him. They surround him with love, trust and conviction.

Failure does not exist for me. Only results do. It is up to us to decide if they are in line with our hopes. If that is the case, great. If it is not, we have to change our tactics. In any event, we will always reach our goal with this mentality, and, in the worst case, we will achieve another one. By constantly imagining the worst case scenario, we create a loser mentality.

By constantly imagining the worst case scenario, we create a loser mentality.

I was on a talk-show a few years ago. I was a guest along with the mother of Tony Parker, the great French professional basketball star. The subject was about children in professional sports. Sports journalists asked the following question: "What would Tony Parker have become if he had not achieved success? Did he have a plan B?" Mrs. Parker answered: "Tony succeeded precisely because he did not imagine failure. It is possible that had he thought of it, he would not have succeeded as he has."

"Tony succeeded precisely because he did not imagine failure. It is possible that had he thought of it, he would not have succeeded as he has."

CHAPTER 4
The winning method

1. THE PLAN

It all starts with a parent's dream, a vision, a crazy gamble, a project.

All great success stories one day start with a vision.

a. Richard Williams' plan

I had the opportunity to meet Richard Williams, the father of the great champions, Venus and Serena Williams, in 2007 during a tournament in Miami. He is one of a kind. He has his strange beliefs and his eccentricities, but he is still a great person. I have always admired people who do not follow the pack, in a world full of people who look the same. We enter new territory with Richard. We talked for a long time, and he told me how, starting with nothing and being completely new to the subject, he gave birth to two of the greatest champions in modern tennis.

Richard Williams came up with the idea of turning his children into tennis champions one weekend at home. Serena and Venus were not yet born, but Richard and Oracene Williams already had two other children.

"Honey, we are going to make two more babies!" said Richard Williams to his wife after learning of the amount of prize-money awarded to the winner of a tennis tournament.

While watching television, he stumbled upon an awards ceremony in a professional tournament. He was stunned when he heard the amount of prize-money awarded to the winner and the losing finalist. The players worked for four days and earned $40,000! The next day he found a newspaper to check that it was not a prank. He then went to his wife and announced: "Honey, we are going to make two more babies!"

His dream was born that day. From that moment on, he threw himself into his project: to program his daughters to become great champions. He planned everything in minute detail, and stuck to the plan with all the discipline and determination needed to carry out such an endeavour.

b. A family project

Richard Williams is just one example of many. Andre Agassi's father had the same dream, as did the fathers of Monica Seles and Maria Sharapova; so too did the father of Tiger Woods, in another discipline. All of these parents decided one day that their child would become a champion and each one has achieved their dream.

How did they go about it? What are the conditions necessary for the accomplishment of such a project? What are the risks? Is it accessible to any parent or must you have exceptional children?

I propose to answer all of these questions by giving you the handbook to success.

c. Give a motivation and a goal to your child

Children's lives are often disconnected from reality. Sometimes, as parents, we try to protect them from it. "They will have enough time to figure it out," we often hear. The children are "protected". We strive to give them a good quality of life and everything we did not have in our own childhood. They are too often the receptacle for our own frustrations.

This behavior is perfectly understandable, but it tends to take responsibility off of the child and not motivate him to do any activity. Why should I make an effort when everything is given to me? Why cook when someone can do it for me? Why bring my plate to the sink? Why make my bed?

These small daily chores are the first steps to understanding the obligations of adulthood: must we not work to survive? It is therefore important to instill these values in our children so that they may find enough motivation in themselves to make the efforts we will ask of them.

It is important to instill these life values in our children so that they may find enough motivation in themselves to make the necessary efforts.

Our first approach will be to explain to them, and then make them clearly understand the stakes in life. We can obtain everything from life, everything we want: happiness, emotions, money, if we fight for it and deserve it.

Richard Williams went even further. He sold his house and moved to the ghetto. He wanted his girls to have the desire to get out of it. He refused to make it easy for them. This is what he told me:

"When she turned six (he is talking about Venus), I wondered what I would do with her and her sister because any child is comfortable in a familiar environment. But it is an entirely other matter in real life, and you must come out of your cocoon in order to perceive your power. So when Venus turned seven, I did the unthinkable. I do not know if you know what the ghetto is really like: people who live on the streets, who do and deal drugs... Me, I took my daughters to the ghetto. One day we found ourselves in the street next to a drunken woman who screamed insanities and who was hitting herself. She looked at Venus and Serena and said: 'Look at the pretty little girls. Mine were like that once, and look at what they have become!' Her daughters looked crazy with disheveled hair, completely scruffy. Bull's eye! They learned everything I tried to teach them from this woman. As of that moment Venus made ambitious life projects and Serena started to comb her hair, she who never

"In the real world, you must come out of your cocoon in order to perceive your power." R. Williams

wanted to touch a comb before... That was all that needed to be said."

Richard was able to make his daughters understand that they could have the lives they wanted if they gave themselves the means, that their lives would be the image they chose to create. He instilled a true motivation in them and offered them a project they agreed with.

2. SELF-PERCEPTION

a. We become the creatures of our minds

"Talent is a dwarf, whereas self-esteem is a giant."
J. Petit-Senn

This means that every one of us is the image our mind reflects back to us. What counts is not reality but the way in which we interpret it. Maybe this seems exaggerated and simplistic, but we experience it every day.

I have seen untalented, but confident people, achieve great things.

I saw many very talented players who were incapable of dominating matches because they did not put themselves in the body of a winner. And I met players, who were considered underdogs, who found the means to dominate matches the results of which have been predicted in advance. I saw fairly untalented, but confident people, achieve great things. I saw people who were told they had a life-threatening disease find the strength to conquer the disease, but also people who wasted immense gifts because they lacked confidence in themselves. I found many unattractive people to be beautiful because of the energy they radiated.

If Paul decides to some handiwork around the house and the result is not as great as he would have hoped, his brain will conclude that he is not gifted. Yet this is false. If he did not succeed the first time, can we really conclude something? By having only tried once? He already does not believe in himself the second time he tries, and his brain sends messages like: "What am I doing here? I am not good at handiwork and I do not like it. It is the weekend and I would better spend my free time doing something else..." The result is expected. He has a second and then a third negative experience with this activity. And the conclusion is the same: "I am horrible at handiwork." So much so that from now on, handiwork has such a negative connotation to him that there is little chance he will reverse the trend.

His perception of things has modified reality. He suggested failure even before it existed.

The problem is that his perception of things has modified his reality. Paul suggested failure even before it existed.

When you think about it, everyone has this type of experience one day or another... If he had addressed the problem of handiwork by thinking that it was his thing, that he was a kind of prodigy, a handy person, better yet, an ultra-creative person in the subject matter, the result would have certainly been different. Destabilizing, no? Especially if we imagine him faced with a small dilemma about how to properly place a mirror, but this time he is full of energy, focused, calm and determined to resolve the problem. Everything would be different. He would find solutions, maybe even invent some. Even if the result may not be professional, he would have invented many solutions to sidestep the problem because his self-confidence would motivate him.

People get discouraged because they think they are incapable of succeeding. Once they think that, there is no use in trying because it will only confirm what they believe: "I am incapable." If we start off with that mind-set, there is no point in going on because it is certain that the outcome will be negative.

It is not who we are that counts, but what we believe we are. For this, you must believe, believe in your future, believe in your capabilities.

I think of Abraham Lincoln, who lost all of his electoral campaigns over almost thirty years before being elected to the highest office: President of the United States of America. He only experienced setbacks. If he had viewed them as such, he obviously would never have kept on trying. No, he always knew that he was capable. When he lost an election, he was satisfied with learning from his setbacks in order to do better the next time.

It is not who we are that counts, but what we believe we are. For this, you must believe, believe in your future, believe in your capabilities.

Venus and Serena Williams' father knows this. He explains that he started by giving his daughters a beautiful image of themselves so that they could see in themselves what he wanted them to become.

You must make the child understand that they are capable of anything, and not set any limit for the accomplishment of his or her dream.

"I understood that the only way to succeed in my endeavour was to make them get it into their heads that they were the strongest in the world, so that they could actually become it. I wanted my daughters to know that they were the greatest champions, that they were better than the others."

Yet, behind this seemingly simple concept lies a reality. Success can only happen if you conceive of it. There is no miracle. Children possess unlimited capabilities. It is the responsibility of the parents to believe in them, to make them aware of them and to use them.

The first step in making a champion therefore entails convincing your child that he or she is one. You must make the child understand that they are capable of anything, and not set any limit for the accomplishment of his or her dream.

b. "No limit"

The only limits are the ones conceived in our minds.

Our mind works constantly. It delivers its concepts by referring to our experiences and those of others which it has integrated as an incontestable fact and which it applies to itself.

The limits we set for ourselves are the only things that stop us from pursuing any field.

This problem is accentuated by the fact that we live in a society that is governed by the notion of what is appropriate. There is acceptable behavior and unacceptable behavior. If our goals fall into the "unacceptable" category, then we will find dozens of people who will explain to us that what we want to do is impossible, that we will not make it, simply because no one has done it up until now.

Thinking that something is impossible because no one has done it before is the worst obstacle to progress. The key to progress resides in surpassing yourself.

This kind of reasoning is the worst obstacle to progress. The key to progress resides in surpassing yourself.

All those people who do not give themselves the means to do things, all those people who limit themselves, who do not believe in themselves or who do not try, are the first to suffer when they see others doing what they were incapable of doing. They are the ones who try to discourage us. You must ignore them because, once again, "Nothing is impossible for a brave heart."

The first and most frequent pitfall of tennis players is to play against a ranking instead of an opponent.

Tennis is definitely not exempt from this rule. Tennis players are the first to build barriers that are unfortunately relayed by their entourage and sometimes by other players. The first and the most frequent pitfall is to play against a ranking instead of an opponent.

This is a fault we find in a lot of tennis players. The player checks out their opponent's ranking. Depending on the ranking, he makes an opinion about their level and his performance is completely influenced by this image of his opponent. Guaranteed failure. Another example: a lot of players think that if they do not work for two days, they need a week's training to get their game level back. All of these mental limitations are very bothersome because it is important to know how to adapt in tennis. How would this same player react if he were forced to stop playing for medical reasons, just two days before the most important match of the year? I doubt that he would be competitive.

The only good result in a tournament is winning it.

That is why I always say to my players: "If you are going to compete in this tournament, it is to win. If not, do not participate." Players and their entourage too often focus on what they consider to be a good result. No. The only good result is victory. The player's entourage is elated when the "little one" gains his first ATP points. He got through the qualifications and a round in the final draw to obtain them. Again no. It is not enough just to obtain his first points. If we think that way, the player will not be able to win the tournament. And what if he is capable of doing so? We have maybe prevented him from winning it with that type of reasoning. We sometimes hear coaches announce in regards to their player: "I am happy if he is in the quarter-finals." How horrible! The only good result in a tournament is winning it.

I remember a coach who sent me a text message before and after his player's matches. I already knew when she would win and when she would lose. It is terrible to say but the match was played out in advance. He was sometimes completely confident in his player, and other times he seemed full of doubt. His influence on his player was such that she had no chance of winning if he did not believe in her that day.

Marcos Baghdatis was the first to make me understand that limits only exist in the mind. That is how he has made me a better person. He was ranked 250th when I started training him and he was participating in a big tournament in Bratislava,

Slovakia. This tournament had considerable prize money: $125,000. He made it to the final where he faced Dominik Hrbaty, who was ranked 14th at the time.

The beginning of the match was completely one-sided. Marcos was tense, the ball did not come off the racket correctly, and Hrbaty was unwavering. That was when I surprised myself by thinking: "Ok, it has been a great tournament! He got through the qualification rounds and reached the final. He will advance well in the rankings." I foresaw his defeat, I visualized it. But the boy I train is a champion, and he did not see it that way. So, he got a grip on himself, hung in and ended up winning in two sets. I learned my lesson! Thankfully for Marcos, I did not outwardly show him what I was feeling. I did not destabilize him. Marcos taught me that I had to believe in him, to believe that he is capable of the greatest feats. He taught me to refuse any limiting belief.

Marcos taught me that I had to believe in him, to believe that he is capable of the greatest feats. He taught me to refuse any limiting belief.

I understood the lesson and he qualified for the Australian Open two months later, only losing to Roger Federer in the last sixteen, after having fought off Ljubicic and Robredo back to back.

Even better, he faced Roger Federer the following year in Doha and lost. After the match he cried tears of deception and I thought: "Everyone believes it is normal to lose to this tennis giant. Players step onto the court just to get a good score. Marcos really came to win. He is different."

Marcos is right. By forcing me to believe in him, he has made me a better coach. For the first time, I am aware that anything is possible. He has taught me a lot about coaching.

By forcing me to believe in him, he has made me a better coach.

The same rules should apply to our children. Whether we are a coach or a parent, we must always avoid setting limits for them. If we think even for an instant that the child is incapable of overcoming a limitation, of winning a tournament, of being stronger than someone else, we run the great risk of this actually being true in reality.

c. Doubt does not exist

Doubt creates evasive behavior.

Doubt is a future champion's number one enemy. Firstly, doubt creates stress, and stress is not a good advisor when decisions need to be made.

The player who doubts develops evasive behavior.

Fear of the future is a deterrent for everyone, but particularly for up-and-coming champions. In order to set ambitious goals and to invest 100% of yourself every day – a requirement if you want to improve and succeed – you must not have doubts. If the player doubts, he or she will systematically develop evasive behavior. They will train indifferently, will be nervous during matches and training sessions, will appear unmotivated during meets or worse, will "chuck the match". All of these unpleasant attitudes are in fact reactions to doubt and anxiety. I often explain to those people who condemn players who behave this way that they must understand what lies behind the behavior. We too often judge the act, rather than try to understand the suffering that provokes it.

Coaches often come to wrong conclusions about a player because of that player's behavior.

Imagine a player who does not give his all during training. An outside observer would conclude that he is lazy. The problem is when this judgment comes from his coach or parents. I had this discussion with a young player from my Academy. He was training without any conviction or personal investment. His coach – whom I subsequently fired – spoke of him in these terms: "He is lazy. He does not give his all, he does not improve." My analysis was different: "He left his country and the family he loves. He wakes up very early in the morning, works very hard physically, and you are explaining to me that he is not motivated! I do not believe that." After getting to know the player more, I have come to understand that doubt prevents him from advancing and giving the best of himself. He is afraid of failure. He just needs to regain self-confidence in order to get back to work and truly blossom.

This error is all too common. We notice a behavior and we come to hasty conclusions. We should not be fatalist. Inadequate behavior can be modified, but you must first try to understand the reasons behind it. Doubt is at the core of the problem most of the time.

It is common for the professional tennis player to doubt because his future is uncertain. Everything he has worked towards can be called into question so he always measures himself to others by way of matches. The player knows that some crushing defeats can be the beginning of a bad period because the defeats make him doubt himself. He also knows that an emphatic victory can buy him some time. That is why each match is very important.

Doubt is the number one enemy. We must fight it.

Doubt leads to defeat.

Doubt is also the number one enemy of a tennis player because it will determine the outcome of matches. Indeed, a match is determined by a few points at key moments. The player who wins those points has a good chance of winning the match. Professional players know how to recognize those decisive moments. In a typical match, there are about three or four times during which the match can turn in favor of one player or the other. Stress and emotions are intense at these moments because victory and/or defeat are right before their eyes. The higher the stakes, the more the emotions are intense, and unfortunately, this affects the game. It tenses the muscles, provokes faults, bad tactical choices and too short a game... The player

The match will be won by the player who has fewer doubts, the one who has the most confidence in his future.

who wins the duel is the one who is able to control and surpass these paralyzing emotions.

The equation is simple. The player who does not doubt or is not afraid of the future will win the match. He is the one who will push back his opponent and the one who will hit the right balls that will lead him to victory.

Champions do not doubt.

Pessimism and negativity are dangerously contagious. You must keep far away from people who send those types of messages.

The first time Rafael Nadal won the French Open, he immediately declared that he had the intention of winning Wimbledon. People in the profession were shocked by this announcement and said that it was impossible, that his game was not adapted to that surface, that he was a wonderful clay court player, but was not sufficiently strong on grass. But Nadal believed that he would win. And he did win the final the following year. We should not be influenced by the barriers others create for us. If we listen to the pessimists, we do not do anything anymore. Pessimism and negativity are dangerously contagious. You must not listen to them and keep as far away from people who send those types of messages. True champions become exactly what they have decided. They set goals and put everything in place to reach them.

Prepare children to not have doubts.

The stakes are high. If you do not want to become, like many players, a victim of the kind of doubt that subjugates and paralyzes you, you must eliminate it. The same method applies to make sure this happens. It all starts with the type of education we give children. The parent's role is to develop self-confidence in the child, to educate them to succeed, and to prevent them from doubting.

Richard Williams told me that he "forbade doubt to enter his home." He himself was banned from doubting, in his acts and his words. He forbade his daughters to even consider failure as a viable option.

Richard Williams told me that he "forbade doubt to enter his home".

Imagine the power this gives you: to have a long-term goal, a daily program and to invest 100% of yourself. If we trust our resources, we always advance knowing that success is at the end of the journey.

d. The power of the mind

"The body follows the mind. We become a champion off the court." Richard Williams

Tennis is a form of expression just like music or literature. You cannot cheat in these fields; you must show who you really are. One of my friends is a businessman who often plays tennis with his clients or associates. In his opinion, it reveals their true nature. To quote his exact words: "That way, I know who I am dealing with."

We step onto a court with our qualities and our faults, our fighting spirit and our psychology. In a word, who we are. We face an opponent who forces us to reveal ourselves. Some have the impression they are fighting to survive. For others, it is a fight for victory. In every case, you bring your own personality to the court.

We step onto a court with our personality. We face an opponent who forces us to reveal who we are.

This personality is developed off the court. Parents help their children develop the mind of a champion.

The mind acts on the body with incredible force. I recently read an enlightening American study carried out on a group of basketball players of the same skill level. Half of the group followed a classic and complete physical preparation. The other half did nothing, but experienced the exercises mentally, however long it took. The researchers noticed that on a scale of 1 to 100, the first group – those who really worked – had progressed by 60. The second group had progressed by 20 even though the players had not done a thing, but their brains still sent a message of effort. This study clearly demonstrates how the mind can act on the system. Anything is possible when you add an impeccable physique to a mind of steel and a positive mentality. All around the world, people achieve things every day that medicine or science believed to be impossible. People who are told they have a life-threatening disease are able to heal by the power of their own will, by ignoring the limits of their body and without burdening themselves with useless questions.

3. THE FAMILY MODEL

a. The family, a conveyor of values

I always tell my colleagues: "If you want to know how these children will turn out, start by observing their parents.

I always tell my colleagues: "If you want to know how these children will turn out, start by observing their parents." This theory has been confirmed in the majority of cases, and not just on a physical level. It also holds true for the personality and the behavior of the child.

A child uses many role models to grow. This can be an enormous asset when we are aware of it and use it wisely.

Children are intelligent. If they see that we ask a lot of them but not the same from ourselves, failure is guaranteed.

That is why I encourage coaches to be good role models. If we want to obtain the best from a child, we have to lead by example. "Do what I say, not what I do" is definitely not the way to be credible. If we want others to follow us, we must be worthy of their trust. Children are intelligent. If they see that we ask a lot of them but not the same from ourselves, failure is guaranteed.

That is why I do not allow my coaches to smoke. They have to set an example. I used to smoke two packs of cigarettes a day. I quit when I decided to become a coach.

When I was training Marcos Baghdatis full-time, when he was then ranked 250th in the world, we decided that he would have to lose some weight because his body could no longer be truly effective with so much extra mass. He was subjected to a drastic diet. It was up to him to respect it. I was loyal and together we followed the nutritional guidelines and he lost 13-15 pounds in three months. I wanted to show him that despite the difficulty, I was able to do as much. I wanted to be loyal. The effort had to be made, so we did it together. Eight months later, despite an arm operation that sidelined him for four months, he became No.80 in the world, and a year later, he played the Australian Open final.

"Embody what you teach and only teach what you embody."[1]

"Embody what you teach and only teach what you embody[1]" is, in my eyes, one of the foundations of coaching. Parents should make it the absolute standard for their children. You must become high-level parents to develop high-level children.

The following is a story taken from "Way of the Peaceful Warrior"[1], which perfectly illustrates the responsibility of the teacher towards his student:

"A mother takes her young son to Mahatma Gandhi. She pleads with him: "Please, Mahatma. Tell my son to stop eating sugar." Gandhi reflects then declares: "Bring your son back in two weeks." Surprised, the woman thanks him and promises to do what he asked of her. Two weeks later, she returns with her son. Gandhi looks the young boy straight in the eyes and says: "Stop eating sugar." Thankful but stunned, the woman asks him: "Why did you ask me to bring him back in two weeks?

1. Dan Millman "Way of the Peaceful Warrior"

You could have told him the same thing the first time I came." Gandhi replies: "Two weeks ago, I was eating sugar."

Children develop in the environment we create for them, with the values we unintentionally teach them because of our own daily behavior. Children observe the reactions of their parents and have a tendency to reproduce them. I remember a player who always blamed the public when matches did not go her way. She accused the public of distracting her and the match was over very quickly. I later learned that her father had the same type of attitude in life. He did not tackle the actual problem to which he was confronted but blamed other people who were not necessarily responsible. He was fighting the wrong fight.

When you launch such an ambitious project for your children, you must impose the same discipline you expect of them on yourself.

We send messages to children without even speaking. If they witness the values, behavior and commitment of a champion, they will have all of the ingredients for success at their disposal.

When you launch such an ambitious project for your children, you must impose the same discipline you expect of them on yourself.

Children always try to imitate their parents. Therefore, you must present them with a model that is accordance with what you want them to become.[2]

b. Family involvement: love and support

Once tennis parents completely invest in their children, they are very often severely criticized. I witness this every day in my professional life. The same, seemingly harmless questions arise: "Do you not think that parents live vicariously through their children?", "Are children not a tool for their parents' success?"

---

2. For more details, see Chapter 4.4 : Values in professional tennis

These questions are actually frontal attacks and often reflect frustration. Our society has evolved. Last century, a baker's son became a baker. Parents passed on their passion and knowledge to their children. This was an integral part of their duty towards them. They invested all the necessary time to pass on, train and teach. Their initial professional goal was centered on personal success, and later it transformed into a family project with their child at its core.

Today, the child must grow up not only with references given at home, but also in school, daycare or at the baby-sitter.

Today the situation is completely different. Parents are generally busy working to provide for the family. Children are not only raised by their parents. They must develop at home, in school, in daycare or with a baby-sitter. Parents leave the school the heavy responsibility of educating their children, of teaching them a profession and of passing on values. The child must therefore grow up with references given by others.

Let us get back to tennis parents. What is their role? They teach, accompany and train their child in an activity. But above all, they dedicate almost all of their time to their child's success. There is nothing wrong with this. They give everything they can, and in doing so, they take complete responsibility for their child's future.

The winning method requires genuine implication of the parents at their child's side.

The winning method requires genuine implication of the parents at their child's side. The road is long. It requires patience, work, self-sacrifice, perseverance, and the child will accomplish even more if he receives love. He asks to be supported throughout the achievement of his professional project. He needs a daily loving presence. He needs a role model who gives the necessary energy, a positive and optimistic person to help him during difficult times.

I often say that parents who apply these rules are better coaches for their children. A parent communicates best with their child. Parents are always more determined than a coach because it involves their child.

c. The importance of a team and the role of each team member

The winning formula resides in teamwork. No one can succeed alone. There has to be a winning trio: the player, the parent and the professional.

Each one has a very precise role to play within the common project. Parents must create the mind-set by respecting the values of the professional world. They must fuel the child's motivation and support him every day.

The coach must provide the technical, tactical, and physical weapons so that the child can develop his game harmoniously.

The child grows with the help of guides: one is a spiritual guide; the other is a technical one. But it is above all the passion that will be put into the instruction of each that will make the child improve at a faster pace.

In his book, Brad Gilbert, the former coach of Andre Agassi and Andy Roddick, explains how roles were distributed between team members when he was a professional tennis player.

"My grandfather was a good listener. He was a quiet man. In many respects, he was very different from my father, who was obsessed with one thing – tennis – and tried desperately to strengthen my motivation.

Chiv[3] reminded me a lot of my grandfather. Quiet, easy-going, with no prejudices. He always listened. He never asked me indiscreet questions, but if I told him that I was having problems with a girl, he listened to me and gave me advice."

To have a strong team, each team member must find their own place within it so that the child can find an answer to all of his needs.

Being part of a team means working well together, knowing each other's strengths and weaknesses, using them in the

3. *Chiv was his coach at the time.*

best way, trusting and building together for the benefit of the child.

4. VALUES IN PROFESSIONAL TENNIS

a. Work

Too much comfort is the number two enemy of a future champion because it creates complacency. However, frustration and envy are ideal detonators for effort. The equation is relatively easy to understand: if your child has everything, he will not want anything. They will not make an effort if they do not want anything.

You must, as Richard Williams did, avoid any excess of material and psychological comfort. The life of a champion is a daily work in progress. What is true today is not always true tomorrow. I have to get what I want by the sweat of my brow. I have to earn it. Nothing lasts forever, everything must be acquired through effort. For example: if I want to eat, I must be able to set the table, to cook, then to clear the table and do the dishes. It is a mistake to call the children once food has been put on the table and lunch is served. The message is clear. Unfortunately, ready-made does not exist in life. Children must be raised with that state of mind.

Ready-made does not exist in life. Children must be raised with this state of mind.

b. Adaptation

Tennis is first and foremost a sport of adaptation. Only the rules and the desire to win are set in stone. The rest fluctuates constantly. Game conditions can change radically from one day to the next: the slow surface can become quick, the spins on the balls can change. The balls are softer or harder than the day before. Altitude influences the height and length of balls and requires that racket tension be modified in order to obtain more control or speed. Wind, sun, and humidity also affect the nature of the ball.

The opponent possesses different strengths and tries to make things difficult for you. Powerful, deft, determined, talented, brilliant, solid, with a good forehand, a good backhand, a serve-and-volleyer or a baseline player, offensive or defensive. The player must quickly adapt and find solutions to win.

Players have a better chance of reaching a high level if they adapt to different situations.

All of the principles tied to these two basic rules are summarized in the 8 steps to excellence which define the values of professional tennis.

c. 8 steps to excellence

Reaching a level of excellence in any field is a question of psychology. I have defined 8 steps to excellence in order to outline the psychology that is needed to reach a very high level. These 8 steps describe the process, the values and mind-set of high performance.

"The future belongs to those who believe in the beauty of their dreams."
Anna Eleanor Roosevelt

1. HAVE A VISION :
ALL GREAT SUCCESS STORIES START WITH A VISION
It starts with a dream. A dream you decide to make a reality. This is how all legends are born. We call it "Vision" because it does not remain a dream. Once it has become tangible it becomes a source of inspiration. It casts us into the future. From that moment on, "the path is laid out", as the popular saying goes.

This vision is located at the very top of the value system, like something that seems unattainable in the eyes of others but exemplifies the most desired wish of the dreamer.

2. FOLLOW YOUR BELIEFS :

SILENCE THE WORLD AROUND YOU AND LISTEN TO WHAT YOUR SOUL IS TELLING YOU. FOLLOW WHAT YOU HEAR RIGHT AWAY!

We all have a certain idea of our abilities, our qualities, of what pushes us and repels us... We project our hopes in the future. We know our faults, we know what needs to be perfected and the people who will be able to guide us in our Vision. Many answers are buried inside of us. We must listen to them, understand them and then follow them.

"The two obstacles between a man and his dreams are the lack of will and the absence of faith."
Richard M. Devos

3. SET GOALS :

ON THE PATH TO YOUR VISION, FIND THE PORTS WHERE YOU CAN ANCHOR YOURSELF.

Vision is the final goal to be reached. Beacons must be positioned as reference points on this long journey through the execution of daily goals. This reassures us and allows us to verify that we are on the right path. By adhering to a daily mission, we take another step towards our goal every day.

"Obstacles are those frightful things you see when you take your eyes off your goal."
Henry Ford

4. WORK HARD :

THE WORK IS JUST BEGINNING FOR YOU ONCE OTHERS BECOME EXHAUSTED.

When we like to work, to feel the pleasure of improving at each moment, when we delight in feeling our body become tired by the effort, when we love perfection and strive for it constantly, then we advance faster than others and have a feeling of accomplishment that will lay the foundation for self-confidence.

"Genius begins great works; labor alone finishes them."
Joseph Joubert

5. HAVE THE RIGHT ATTITUDE :

TO BECOME A CHAMPION, YOU MUST FIRST HAVE THE ATTITUDE OF A CHAMPION.

What distinguishes an average player from a very good player is in large part his attitude. It is also what distinguishes a very good player from a champion. Your attitude in sports is important for it is all you have left when your game abandons you. Attitude shows the true face of the player and betrays his mental conditioning when faced with an opponent. The player's attitude can save him when he is being dominated on the court. Working on attitude is an important step to forging self-confidence. The player's attitude only depends on him! It is up to him to develop in order to hold his head up high when leaving a court

"Great people have determination; weak people have only desires."
Chinese proverb

6. FIGHT TO WIN :

THE MOST BEAUTIFUL VICTORY IS THE ONE WE WIN ON A BAD DAY, AT THE EXPENSE OF A WEAKER PLAYER.

When a player steps onto the court to play a match, winning must be his only goal.

Basically, the quality of his game does not matter much. The beauty of the performance is found in his results, and in the ability to find the road to victory including days when nothing goes his way.

Do not fight the wrong fight. When we step onto the court, we only have one enemy: ourselves; and only one way to fight that enemy: accept the fact that you may not be brilliant that day, but fight to win.

"Nothing we can do can change the past, but everything we do changes the future."
Ashleigh Brilliant

7. DARE TO FACE IT :

HE WHO DARES BELIEVES. HE WHO DARES ACTS. HE WHO DARES PUTS ALL HIS ENERGY INTO HIS DREAM.

In most cases, a match is often won by the player who has dared: dared to play his game, dared to set the pace, dared

"Your actions speak so loudly that I cannot hear what you are saying."
Ralph Waldo Emerson

to show his desire to win. A tennis match is a metaphor for life. To not dare is the same as disowning yourself, like kowtowing to someone else's domination. The journey of a champion is paved with courage, the courage to claim who he is, what he is pursuing and fighting to obtain.

8. NEVER GIVE UP :
NO ONE CAN MAKE YOU FAIL... ONLY YOU CAN MAKE YOURSELF FAIL IF YOU ACCEPT DEFEAT
All great champions are great fighters. Their personality is molded and strengthened by the difficulties they encounter and their capacity to overcome them. You must rejoice in the difficulties that arise because adversity makes you grow.

"Good wood does not grow easily.
The stronger the wind, the stronger the tree."
Chinese proverb

5. PRACTICE: A TYPICAL DAY WITH A PLAYER

Here is a practical guide outlining what the advisor must accomplish on a daily basis to obtain effective programming.

a. What should be done each day?

– Instill self-confidence in the child: give him love, a lot of love, and attention. Give the child self-esteem every day, compliment his performance in every field. Make him feel how much you are proud of his strengths.

– Instill the values of professional tennis in him, as they appear in the 8 steps to excellence. These values must be completely integrated. You must always emphasize work, commitment, and tenacity. Make the child understand that everything in life is earned; he has to make an effort to get what he wants.

You must emphasize work, commitment, and tenacity.

– Be an example. You must always remember that the parent remains a role model. The child reproduces your gestures, your mentality, and integrates what you do. You must be positive, ambitious, hard-working and tenacious.

– Be serene: if positive or negative events occur in the short-term, the long-term project must never be questioned. Do not let pessimism, or even worse, defeatism, get the upper hand.

– Never set limits. Anything is always possible as long as the mind does not put barriers in your way.

b. What should be done during training sessions?

– Work hard, very hard. Maintain a high concentration level as long as possible. When the focus wears off, take a break, because the work will no longer be effective. The child should not get in the habit of giving only 50% of himself. Respect the child's rhythm.

These small, daily successes establish self-confidence and high-level values.

– Put the player in a successful situation. Let him succeed gradually by placing the bar very high. These small, daily successes establish self-confidence and high-level values. If the player does not succeed the first time, that is not a problem. It will teach him to work harder to obtain what he wants. Do not pay attention to how much time goes by or to the number of unsuccessful attempts. The important thing is to get a result.

– Have the right attitude: maintain the desire in the child by being enthusiastic, optimistic and passionate. Always remain calm but dynamic. If the child does not succeed, ask yourself the right questions and find a solution so that he can obtain the results expected of him. Everything depends on the advisor's attitude and on the advice he or she gives to the child. You must be creative.

c. What should I do before matches?

The tennis match is an opportunity for the player to test his skills. It is a moment of truth that will reveal how much he has improved. A match is too often a source of stress for players who lack self-confidence; the pre-match pep talk is a step that should not be neglected. The attitude of the player's entourage greatly determines the final result.

The child must face the match with clear, simple and achievable goals, the results of which only depend on him.

– Have a clear speech prepared beforehand. Right before the match, explain to the child that he can win or lose. The most important thing is that he should have the attitude of a champion. A champion never gives up, a champion fights to get what he wants. There is a chance that he may lose the match, but in most cases, he wins.

– Be serene and confident when game day approaches: "You will win because you are the best." Whomever the opponent (higher or lesser ranked, tall, short, younger, or older), your child is always the best.

– The child must face the match with clear, simple and achievable goals, the results of which only depend on him. He must concentrate on these goals and forget about his opponent. Again, he controls the results.

d. What should I do during matches?

– An attitude: remain very calm. Do not show any emotions that are likely to show a lack of confidence or a hint of doubt on your part. Reassure the child with positive gestures.

During matches, do not show any emotions that are likely to show a lack of confidence or a doubt on your part.

– A speech: use words that bring about confidence: "You are doing the right things", "You are a champion." If the need arises, encourage him: "It is alright, hang on", "It will pass, continue." Encourage him to get aggressive: "Fight", "Do not give up."

e. What should I do after the matches?

– If the child wins: show your joy, but not too much. You are happy, but you consider the victory to be normal. He is the best, so he won.

After defeats, the advisor and the coach must make the child feel that he has the right to make mistakes.

– If the child loses: how you handle defeat is important because the way the child experiences it influences the way he will approach future matches. The child's ability to be competitive in a match highly depends on the way parents make him experience defeat. Post-loss is a difficult moment for parents and coaches. They have gone through a lot of stress during the match, and were unable to release any of the pressure. Post-match comments often become an outlet for expressing their feelings.

You should not dramatize the situation. Do not show that you are disappointed. Be loyal. Focus on the positive right away. Do not reproach the child. He has the right to make errors. He is also learning a lot during these moments and must feel that he has the right to make mistakes.

6. THE 7 COMMANDMENTS OF COACHING

a. I believe in my player in any situation

The coach is a guide. He indicates routes, marks checkpoints, and provides the energy necessary to succeed

Whether he sets out to or not, he leaves an imprint on the player through tactical, technical, and physical choices but also through the words he speaks and the importance he gives to things.

The only limits we have are the ones we set for ourselves...

Believing in his player means believing in his potential, in his capacity to go in the right direction, in his strengths and in his exceptional qualities. These are the essential prerequisites to a successful partnership.

We are the image we believe ourselves to be.

That is why the coach must always see the child as a great player. He will in turn influence the child's view of himself.

The coach all too often sets limits for his player: "If you get to the quarter finals, you have fulfilled your contract." Or "You cannot do this or that for the moment."

Result: the player will never surpass the limits set by the coach, even if he has the capacity... The best option is to never even think about limits.

This is a universal principle: anything is possible if you believe it.

b. I only pursue one goal: performance

My way of thinking and philosophy have often led people to think that I acted more as an educator than as a coach and that I strove for the player's comfort... I only have one goal, performance at the highest level. I merely use the most adapted techniques and the tools that work.

I only have one goal, performance at the highest level. I merely use the most adapted techniques and the tools that work.

We must never lose sight of this goal despite numerous factors that are likely to distract us:

– Environmental influences: in the tennis community, like anywhere, most players are average players. This is also true for coaches, and for the majority of people who are part of this environment. Mediocrity is a very contagious disease and the only way to fight against it is by always remembering your goal.

"Habit is either the best of servants or the worst of masters."
Nathaniel Emmons

– Psychological support for the player: the inner mind of a player is a theater of anxieties, fears, and suffering. The first reaction would be to help the player on a human level. But this is not our role. Our job is to make him competitive when he holds a racket. This does not mean that we should ignore his well-being, but we must be careful not to stray from our mission.

– Lassitude: accompanying a player every day is a true challenge because a routine sets in and leads to a certain lassitude: training, travel, hotels, tournaments... Watch out for habit since it can make us lose sight of the goal and dampen our will.

c. I take responsibility for the good and bad results. I question my methods.

I am loyal to my player.

A coach who delights in his protégé's good results, or a player who denounces his coach's inadequacies having lost a match are both behaving deplorably.

I question my methods.

The coach is **RESPONSIBLE** in victory and euphoria, but also in defeat and turmoil. We do not jump a sinking ship. Certainly, if the results disappoint, we most likely have to change something about the player's behavior. That is the role of the coach. If we do not do this, then we are responsible.

We are working together and we must bear the results together: the player and us. We must become one. It is never entirely the fault of this or that part of the whole. We must take responsibility and find the solutions together.

Instead of incriminating the player, the coach must question his own methods: "If we find ourselves in this situation, it is probably because I did not do what was necessary, that I missed something along the way, that I did not succeed in guiding my player in this direction." This is constructive reasoning. There is no shame in making a mistake if we gain in experience and an advantage.

d. I do not judge my player: behavior does not define a person

The coach who judges his player only reveals his own inability to find solutions to the problems facing him.

A coach may at times disapprove of some of his student's behavior, which he deems to be out of place in a high-level competition or just unpleasant.

Some players become enraged during matches, throwing their racket and screaming at the public. Others seem perfectly indifferent to the stakes of the match and make no effort to win.

It is important to understand what lies behind this behavior. It is too easy to label someone as crazy, lazy or lethargic. This type of judgment never deals with the problem.

The golden rule is therefore to never judge your players and never try to define them by their behavior. Excessive behavior is very often a reaction to a stimulus. If the reaction is out of place, it should be corrected.

The player will lose confidence in his coach and in himself if he feels judged, and his results will immediately suffer.

e. I enter the inner world of the player

If I were named president of a large company tomorrow, my first act would not consist of making decisions. In my opinion, this would be the best way to commit errors and to make my future colleagues doubt my capacities.

Understand and master in order to make the right decision.

No, my first act would be to make the most detailed and complete report on the state of the company: what sector is the company in, what is the market for this sector, who are the competitors, the stakes, the lobbying groups, what is the company culture, etc. There are countless questions and the responses are key to a solid understanding of the strategies that should be taken to run the company successfully.

We must have the exact same approach when it comes to sports coaching. It is dangerous to make any decisions before making a complete analysis of the player. This "audit" of the player must focus on his type of game, his qualities, his weaknesses, his physical abilities and psychology.

This last point is especially important for it is often neglected. It will determine the quality of communication between the student and the coach.

Each person has his own vision of things; each person perceives the world in his own way.

One of the coach's first acts must be to enter the inner world of the player, to understand his general perception of the world, and the tennis world in particular.

It is a rare and challenging feat but a necessary one. The coach must be able to see through the player's eyes, to listen with his ears and think with his mind. It is the absolutely essential condition for good communication.

The coach can only truly act when he has a clear view of the players' inner world.

f. I use the proper speech

Use the right speech and words to each of your players.

We sometimes do not measure the weight of our words. We do not realize the effects they produce in the listener. Once we open our mouths, each word is filled with meaning and inevitably provokes a reaction.

So, as a coach, it would be wise to weigh each of our words in order to obtain the desired effect.

We all react differently to stimuli; we each have our own vocabulary. "It is nice out" for a Parisian signifies "It is not raining", whereas for a Marseillais it means "There is not a cloud in the sky and it is 86°F."

To get our messages across, it is best to use a vocabulary adapted to each person.

Customized speech for each situation.

At times you must restore confidence, at other times, comfort or provoke... You must adapt your speech to what the player is going through, the next goals that need to be achieved and the desired outcome.

g. I never react emotionally

A coach must have hindsight and must weigh his words, his reactions and his body language.

We too often see coaches, enraged after a defeat, dump all of their frustration during a "post-match debriefing". Unfortunately, this tradition is an opportunity for the coach to "calm his nerves" which have been put to the test during the match. The effect is, of course, disastrous. The player finds himself drowned in a pool of negativity which has been added to the disappointment of losing a match. The player has not learned anything, but he has lost a bit of that self-confidence that was so difficult to acquire. As for the coach, he does not become any more credible in the eyes of the player.

A coach who reacts emotionally is not acting as a coach, but as a human being who is a victim to his passions.

This is just an example but there are countless others. The coach is a human being and every human being falls prey to his passions. To avoid finding oneself in this type of scenario, the coach should never react emotionally. He should take a step back, wait and always act with a level head.

Part three

PUT TO THE TEST

CHAPTER 5
The absence of method

1. NATURAL SELECTION

Few parents have a winning method, despite the fact that there is proof that it works. A few of the most striking examples: Venus and Serena Williams (fourteen Grand Slam titles) and Tiger Woods (the greatest golf champion in history). Three exceptional champions who know what they are capable of. I do not believe in luck: when we apply ourselves to the winning method, we always obtain the results we expected.

In the majority of case, the children have mass, dense and uncontrolled programming imposed on them.

But the majority of ambitious tennis parents apply a completely different method which is a method in name only. Like some methods, based on fierce natural selection – a large number of players are subjected to the same difficult physical and mental training, and only the strongest survive – the children have mass, dense and uncontrolled programming imposed on them. They are subjected to intense stress since they are the driving force behind their parents' dreams and are the future financial saviors of the entire family. The child runs the risk of paying dearly for a journey that has a good chance of finishing in disaster.

Families are often sacrificed at the altar of success.

Natural selection takes precedence in the absence of a winning method. It is often the most talented, strongest, and toughest characters who make it through. The others disappear and the families are often sacrificed at the altar of success.

2. THE TRIANGULAR RELATIONSHIP

a. The player

Faced with reality

Tennis players are heroes, in my opinion. They are exceptional human beings who have been gifted with remarkable courage. They practice one of the most difficult professions I know. They have no other choice but to excel in an extremely competitive environment (about a hundred players actually earn a living compared with the hundreds of thousands who try their luck). And they face reality without a mask and go before an unsympathetic judge: the match. The players are men and women who face up to their responsibilities and their existence every day. Everything they do and who they are is called into question during every match. Their lives comprise stress, doubt, constant self-questioning, whether they are beginners or Top 10 players.

In my opinion, tennis players are heroes.

Champions often think that the pressure is off once they reach the heights of the world rankings, but, in reality, it gets even worse, because once at the top, they are judged even more since they are more exposed.

Tennis is a microcosm. In the junior categories, all the children and parents know each other, and everyone judges each other. Everyone does their best not to disappoint, to assume the qualities people see in them, to assert their ambitions, and to justify the hopes which have been placed in them.

The expectations of an entire family.

It is the same process whether you are judged by five people in the early years or a million people at the height of your career. You must always develop in the knowledge that everyone is watching. And the way your family views you is the most difficult thing to deal with. Beyond their victories and defeats, a good number of players are responsible for an entire family that has placed all its hopes in them.

You should always listen to the advice of other people.

In 2005, I welcomed a 13-year-old foreign player to my Academy. Her parents had left their country with their four children to travel around Spain to find a professional who could help them make the most of their daughter's talent. They had been searching for a year and a half when I agreed to help them.

Potential

Everything is more complicated when children have not been programmed. They constantly feel insecure because they do not have the necessary self-confidence to reach a very high level.

I have always believed that when you meet an extraordinary person, you know it right away.

When I have to choose players, I study their potential. I look for something rare, en exceptional state of mind, a strong personality or unique game skills. It is often obvious. I have always believed that when you meet an extraordinary person, you know it right away. Sometimes it is not that obvious and you must use your intuition.

My method consists of finding players who stand out from the rest. Some are able to develop better speed in their shots, others are different because of their personality. I like players who have exceptional mental conditioning. Marcos Baghdatis radiated an incredible charisma. Mario Ancic, who did not shine with his game, caught my eye because of his fierce competitive spirit.

What makes tennis so captivating is that each player has a chance with strengths that can be diametrically opposed. Tennis is an extremely rich sport, which calls for a multitude of strengths.

What makes tennis so captivating is that each player has a chance.

We can win with a science of the game, very powerful shots, an impeccable physique, by hanging on until the end or by "breaking" an opponent's game. We can be tough or explosive, atypical or traditional. Champions show their unique aptitudes in one of these fields. Each one develops what corresponds to his personality. Agassi literally suffocated his opponent by preventing him from breathing during and between rallies. Sampras was able to raise his game level to unreachable heights. Nadal invented intimidation with his impressive muscle structure, a pre-match ceremony in the locker room and a warrior attitude during matches. He dominates physically, like a boxer who dares his opponent before the fight.

b. The advisor

The framework

The advisor is the family member, a father or mother, who introduced their child to tennis.

The advisor is the family member, a father or mother, who introduced their child to tennis. They accompany, sometimes coach, and in almost every case, demand that the child obtain results.

The advisor does not leave the child a choice: they must win.

In the absence of a clear method, there is no room for self-confidence. The child is encouraged by the family in the name of a sometimes real, sometimes imaginary predisposition.. The results obtained are up and down at best, and the family begins to worry when the player is faced with tough competitors. There is intense pressure from their entourage, and the expectations are enormous. Faced with these difficulties, parents are often anxious. They have a great fear of the future. Failure is terrible. Oftentimes, everything is banked on this child: the financial future, their credibility vis-à-vis the entourage, a dream of an entire family. Their behavior after each loss is a reflection of their disappointment and the doubts they convey. The advisor does not leave the child a choice: they must win.

The child does not have enough self-confidence to face the project in a serene way. This is normal because the parents themselves are filled with doubts and pass them on to the child every day. Before this uncertain future in which failure is unacceptable, the child tries to hide himself and not deal with what is happening. He gets injured sometimes, he becomes very nervous during training and matches, or even seems to lack aggressiveness during the meets. This is evasive behavior in the face of a stressful match.

The child develops evasive behavior in the face of the stress of a match.

From that moment on, advisors suffers because they feel misunderstood. Their behavior is often excessive. They are ultra-perfectionist, determined, demanding and extremely ambitious in a non-professional world. People in clubs and leagues are generally not very motivated because they only have a vague notion of what professional tennis requires. Therefore, from the beginning, parents are judged and condemned. Conflicts multiply until the inevitable blow-up.

Out of step with the real world, parents are judged and condemned.

As for me, I accept the parents as they are. I respect the work they have done with their child because they are in large part responsible if their child has reached a very good level. They were able to put in place a system that works. Understanding this system gives me the keys to better understanding the player. So, the parents become my partners, I acknowledge them. We have the same objective: to bring their child to the highest level of international tennis. They trust me because I respect them and we can work together to develop our project. Since they trust me, they show their true selves, no matter how excessive, and I can therefore smooth out the edges. I tell them that they have every chance of succeeding if they serve the goal. These parents must change their behavior, even if it requires a

These parents must change their behavior, even if it requires a lot of effort.

lot of effort. If they become better parents, their child will be stronger and their role as advisor will be legitimized and consolidated.

c. The coach

The most difficult profession in the world

The advisor demands results, the coach helps them obtain them.

The advisor demands results, the coach helps them obtain them. He knows that the child wants to and must succeed.

The coach gravitates within the heart of the system. He is an indispensable alchemist who sets the conditions for success at the crossroads of every path. In correlation with the parents, he is also the one who passes on the values of the professional world to the young player. This requires an impressive number of human qualities: be sufficiently self-confident in order to reassure the parents and give them confidence; know how to be captivating and enthusiastic; be sharp in order to detect family issues; prove your discipline every day, and your analytical skills while at the same time being capable of choosing what is essential; be clear when explaining things; know how to be strict but also make yourself lovable. You must overflow with energy and know how to channel it; you must be both a psychologist and a GI; you must educate and also know how to be close to your student. Not simple.

You must overflow with energy and know how to channel it; you must be both a psychologist and a GI; you must educate and know how to be close to your student. Not simple.

The coach's role is essential because everything he says or does has an immediate impact. Talking too much on the court can be harmful; too little, unacceptable. An unfortunate word can make the player lose confidence. Coaching is an art, like a good cooking recipe in which all of the ingredients are perfectly measured out.

Coaching is an art, like a good cooking recipe in which all of the ingredients are perfectly measured out.

This delicate mechanism also requires charisma to handle the authority figure and flexibility to reach out to the player. Coaching entails knowing how to activate the effective levers for each one. It is a fascinating profession because each player is a project and can be considered like a detailed and researched police investigation

Each child is a different book. You must understand everything about them and the stakes they face. You must analyze and synthesize the characteristics that you will use to make them more competitive. There is a lot to study when piecing together the psychological, technical, physical, and tactical levers. And it gets even more difficult, because before discovering the essential (which takes minimum a few months), you must advance haphazardly and you must start working without making mistakes. In other words, we do not yet have the important data but we already have to make decisions and give guidelines.

If ten different coaches work with the same player, they will have ten different diagnoses.

If ten different coaches work with the same player, they will have ten different diagnoses.

If ten coaches make the same diagnosis, they will propose ten different remedies.

And finally if ten coaches must apply the same remedy, they will do it in ten different ways, each with his own personality.

The slightest detail can radically change the outcome. Proper communication is key.

Coaches with no technique quickly become bitter and negative.

It is very difficult to find a good coach because coaching is a complex profession in which people are used to wiping away failures, disenchantment, dismissals, the fact that they have not obtained what they wanted. They often develop a tenacious pessimism and quickly become negative. They nourish many

A good coach knows how to listen and give confidence.

preconceived ideas about things and people. They judge quickly and do not know how to listen or see.

A good coach knows how to listen and give confidence. He is an ally, a big brother who reassures and brings solutions. A good coach is loyal to his player. They become one. Decisions are made together, victories are shared, and so too are defeats.

For the coach, as for the advisor and the player, a lack of trust leads to bad decision-making. As a result, the coach lays the blame on the player when he loses, as if the latter should carry all the responsibility on his shoulders.

There are always solutions to problems.

When I talk to coaches, I notice that they constantly complain about their player: "He does not listen, he does not fight, he plays backwards, he is immature...", the list is long. Worse, this list often leaks to the press. What is the use of having a coach if he cannot find solutions to the problems placed before him? No one is perfect and everyone can improve. We all have qualities and faults.

The coaching profession consists of supporting the strengths of your protégé to make him succeed. If the young player develops ineffective behavior, his coach must find the solutions to make him change it. There are always solutions to problems. If the coach does not find them and complains about the player, he will quickly be replaced by another trainer who will be able to lead that player to victory.

Every behavior exhibited by the player has a meaning.

Let us take for example a harmful behavior that is often found in the most talented players. Since they were little, they have always been told that they possess an amazing talent. They build themselves around this. It is often one of the only positive things they hear because around them, as in tennis in general, people adopt very negative views, especially regarding their losses.

The worst thing that can happen to these people is that their exceptional abilities are called into question, and that overnight, people stop telling them that they have an immense talent. This results in destructive self-defensive reactions. When they risk losing to a less talented opponent, they fear that people are questioning their abilities. They prefer to not face reality: they chuck the match. It is the perfect alibi: they lose, but in a way, they did not try to win. Worse, people tell them: "Yes, you lost, but if you hadn't chucked, you'd have crushed him. You have so much more talent than him." This type of thinking means that we encourage their attitude.

When players doubt their ability to succeed, rather than face reality and run the risks of losing their reputation and their confidence, they evade the problem.

Why do they do this if they have the means to win the majority of their matches and to succeed in life? It is simply because they do not have enough self-confidence. They doubt their ability to succeed, instead of facing reality. At the risk of losing their reputation and their confidence, they flee.

What does a coach do in such a situation? He gives his player the order to stop chucking. And he tries to get his point across any which way, from the "good friend" to the "threatening enemy". The coach neither says that the behavior is dreadful nor makes any effort try to understand it. The result? Nothing. It could even make matters worse. Because the player who chucks is the unhappiest person in the world. He shows complete indifference, but in reality, in the locker-room, he is disgusted with himself, revolted, destroyed. He would have loved to have won that match.

A player who "chucks a match" is the unhappiest person in the world.

As for the coach, he does not stop there. He is frustrated and needs to let off steam. He tells the player that he is lousy, weak, incapable of handling the pressure... I have witnessed this many times... He turns on the losing machine.

The coach must gain the player's trust

When a conflict arises between a player and a coach, I always listen to the player because I assume that his coach should have gained his trust. If that is not the case, we need to understand why.

A journalist who followed my Academy players for a documentary film took me aside one day in Miami. He was shocked by the temperamental, even outrageous, attitude of one of our young female players towards her coach on court. "Look," he told me. "Here are the limits to your system. By listening too much to your players, they end up doing what they want. They become spoiled children. You let them change coaches whenever they want to." To which I replied, "You're saying that to me because you haven't understood. When a player behaves like that, I'm the first not to accept it. Lack of respect and excessive behavior with adults cannot be accepted. However, I want to look beyond that and understand what's fueling that behavior. It's a cry for help from a girl who's hurting and who doesn't believe in her coach. If this is the case, she has no chance of succeeding because she never does anything he suggests wholeheartedly. I've never seen a player respect a coach he's mistreated by. These problems are often an indicator of bad player/coach communication. If I don't listen to a player, if I know that he and his coach will slowly enter a spiral of defeat. The relationship is destructive for both of them. It must end for the common good."

If I do not listen to the player, if I know that he and his coach will slowly starting losing matches.

Coaches at the Academy

At the Academy, as elsewhere, I have had my lot of bad coaches. People who are convinced they are rocket scientists, who are incapable of listening and adapting to their protégés. It took me years to find the proper method that could guarantee

At the Academy, as elsewhere, I have had my lot of bad coaches. People who are convinced they are rocket scientists, who are incapable of listening and adapting to their protégés.

a group of competitive, honest and reliable coaches in the long term. After many disappointments, I finally decided to train a group of young coaches, to select them according to their potential, and to make them become warriors of coaching, thus applying the same method that I use when selecting my players.

The first quality he must have is unwavering determination. His dream must be to succeed professionally, to lead his player to compete in Grand Slam finals. This determination is important if you spend dozens of hours a day on the tennis court and sacrifice your private life in favor of incessant travel around the globe.

The second quality he must have is knowing how to communicate. Coaching is a profession founded on relationships with people. The player must love his coach and this affection must be reciprocated for the relationship to be constructive.

The player must love his coach and this affection must be reciprocated for the relationship to be constructive.

They must love spending time together because they will become inseparable. Without love, it is guaranteed failure. Together, the player and the coach will have to deal with difficult moments, overcome enormous hurdles, and bear disappointments. The secret is to become one body, to understand one another and finally to win together.

What is important is not what we do but the strength of conviction we put into it.

That is why the coach must possess natural charisma. There are people we like right away, with whom we have "a feeling"; and there are others whom we find more difficult to like. There are those whom we want to listen to and those who bore us once they open their mouths. What is important is not what we do but the strength of conviction we put into it.

The idea is to rapidly find the keys to winning. Everything is much easier when we win.

The training week with my coaches is completed with practical follow-up throughout the year. I train them to listen, to analyze, to synthesize, to make decisions, to communicate, and to act.

The idea is to rapidly find the keys to winning. Everything is much easier when we win.

You must work with a first, rapid analysis in order to put in place a winning dynamic. This will allow you to have more time to make a second, deeper analysis in order to go even further.

3. POWER STRUGGLES WITHIN THE TRIANGULAR RELATIONSHIP

There are three main actors in the classic system of tennis: an advisor who puts the pressure and motivates, a coach who gives the keys and confidence, a player who fights to survive in a difficult world and who suffers when he loses confidence in himself but continues the combat.

This little world lives in an unstable balance where everything can be called into question at any moment. The matches regulate each one's mood, bringing a glimmer of hope or nourishing doubts and worries. Victories bring their small batch of joy and the feeling that everything is possible again. Losses are destructive. They erase all hope in one instant, they foster self-questioning, doubts, insecure feelings, and sometimes even despair.

When a player improves rapidly and success is close at hand, you often hear on the part of advisors and/or coaches, in the place of: "Shut up and work!", "Yes, you're right, I understand."

When a player improves rapidly and success is close at hand, he is invariably courted by everyone, sometimes by famous people, wealthy people, powerful people... so much so that this lessens the strength of his entourage.

This presents two key problems:

– The player listens less to his entourage. He loses confidence in his coach. Indeed, the views he hears all around him, especially from prestigious people who claim to perfectly know the subject, make him doubt his inner circle. In the majority of cases, the player becomes withdrawn and stops listening to the advice of those who educate him.

– the advisor and coach are filled with panic at the notion of losing the player at such a beneficial time. They even fear that they will be dismissed. They thus develop "pandering" behavior in regards to the player, and you often hear in the place of: "Shut up and work!", "Yes, you're right, I understand."

There is therefore a swing in the balance of power from the coach and advisor to the player. When we think about it, it is a predictable development, even logical: the child becomes an adult and takes flight. But, in the present case, we have also invested everything in the child for fifteen or twenty years at the price of enormous sacrifice. He is also carrying the dreams of his inner circle. To see him spread his wings and reject his advisor in the moment of truth is difficult to accept! And yet, the first "small victories" are very often the starting point of these kinds of difficulties.

So, the advisor and the coach enter a power struggle the objective of which, admitted or not, is to keep a tight hold on the player. This triangular relationship is ambiguous. The player is in the middle and the roles are confused.

a. When the advisor takes on the role of coach

When the advisor takes on the role of coach, he gives, different, sometimes contradictory, advice to the player. This is not an ideal situation for the player who is caught in the middle.

There are times when the advisor takes on the role of a coach, often because he has doubts, and he has a hard time managing his fear of failure. This constant anxiety makes him act out of panic.

Rather than relay his doubts and questions to the coach, he consults directly with the player, thus discrediting the coach in the eyes of the child. "If I give tennis advice to my son, it is because the coach is not doing so. If I give different advice, it is because he is not capable of doing it himself." This results in the ultimate frustration for a coach who interprets this attitude as a lack of trust. "If the player's father trusts me, why does he give advice in my place?"

The coach feels that his methods are being called into question. It gets even worse when the advisor gives different, and sometimes contradictory, advice to the player. Not exactly an ideal situation for the player who is often caught in the middle, pulled from both sides. Whatever happens, one of the two is unhappy.

If information is not getting through clearly, the results cannot be up to par. In this case, the coach ends up complaining to the advisor and blames the absence of results on the incompetence of the advisor who constantly diffuses false information.

In my opinion, only the coach has the capacity to advise and guide the player because he takes responsibility for both good and bad results.

The player finds himself in the worst situation: the advisor who hired the coach, thus implicitly validating his competence, suddenly decides to take responsibility for the child, and then questions his choice by giving contradictory advice. How do you expect the child to understand what is going on?

Result: the player is confused and the coach is unmotivated.

You must understand one thing: the tennis world is full of know-it-alls. In my opinion, only the coach has the capacity to advise and guide the player because he takes responsibility for both good and bad results. This implies that each decision is weighed and given serious thought. It also implies that he assumes responsibility for everything.

In practice, he can and must refer to the advisor who is his employer. He must inform, explain and make him validate his technical, tactical, physical choices... He will thus always act in the best interest of the player. This is obviously not the case for other people, who give their opinion without being asked, and who do not bear the consequences.

In the case of the advisor, the situation is a bit different since he is also closely involved with the player. The coach will take responsibility for the results, and will be fired if he does not reach his objectives.

b. When the coach takes on the role of advisor

A coach can also take on the role of advisor. The close relationship between the coach and the player can make the coach consider the human being and their life choices as his responsibility. He questions the actions of the advisor and opposes his handling of things. This kind of situation is much more frequent than we think.

Since the advisor's behavior is often excessive and the relationship between a coach and his player very deep, the emotional relationship that develops between them can lead to this type of problem. Watching the player suffer, the coach has a tendency to take sides and oppose the advisor. He considers, correctly or incorrectly, that the advisor must do things differently. The player feels it, and, once again, he finds himself in the middle of a power struggle. Not good...

This is a serious professional error on the part of the coach. Thinking that he is acting in the best interest of the player, he actually puts him in a delicate situation. The child finds himself torn between a professional whom he trusts and his advisor whose legitimacy cannot be called into question. He loses his bearings.

Overstepping his role and taking the side of the player by challenging the advisor is a serious professional error on the part of the coach.

The coach is always the loser in this situation because in the short term, he finds himself in an awkward situation with the player. The coaching profession is difficult and a coach sometimes goes through periods in which his competence, his effectiveness or just the quality of his relationship with the player is questioned. During these periods, the advisor's support is key to ensuring the continuity of his work and the eventuality that the "storm will pass". If he cuts himself off from the advisor, these periods of doubt are fatal.

c. Questioning authority

Once the player feels that there is a divergence of opinions at the top of the power chain, he uses it as an opportunity to find an escape.

Once the player feels that there is a divergence of opinions at the top of the power chain, he uses it as an opportunity to find an escape. He does not fight for victory anymore. He views it as a frightening goal, risky and too uncertain. He adopts one of the many evasive attitudes we described above.

A certain Stanley Milgram, an American social psychologist, performed a now famous experiment on the principle of submission to authority, which perfectly illustrates my point.

A well-known laboratory publishes an ad looking for candidates to participate in memory tests. Many people hurry to the doors of the laboratory due to the compensation the ad had promised. They are greeted by two men in white coats and are then led to a large room. The two scientists, one of whom is a famous doctor, explain the experiment to them: they must determine if a negative stimulus can help improve an individual's memory.

The first individual, whom we will call Mr. A, is seated and attached to a chair. Electrodes are placed all over his body and connected to a monitor. The other individual, Mr. B, is behind the monitor, at the commands.

One of the men in white reads aloud a list of thirty words and thirty adjectives associated with these words. For example: ocean - blue; thought - vague; path - tortuous... Then, the words are chosen at random, and Mr. A must remember the adjective associated with it. Every time Mr. A answers incorrectly, Mr. B must send electroshocks of increasing intensity.

The test begins. Mr. A answers incorrectly. After a slight hesitation, Mr. B sends the first electroshock. Little by little, the mistakes multiply, as do the electroshocks and their intensity. After half an hour, Mr. A cannot take anymore. Completely stressed, sweating, stuttering, he begs Mr. B to stop the torture. The experiment is so real that Mr. B is completely lost. He turns to the men in white coats and asks: "What should I do?" They order him to continue. After a slight hesitation, Mr. B sends a 160-volt electroshock to Mr. A, who screams in pain.

The test continues. The man in white asks: "Time..." No response from Mr. A, who seems completely resigned. Then, he tries: "Rainy?"

"Concentrate!" Mr. B says, very worried. "It isn't complicated!"

"I beg of you, sir!" screams Mr. A. "I am in pain. I want to stop. Please, help me." Mr. B again turns to the man in white, his face completely crestfallen. But he receives the same instruction: "Continue."

We refer to a supreme authority figure in order to escape our responsibilities.

At that moment, a second man in white enters the room. The mood is heavy. He asks his colleague: "Is everything alright?"

"Yes, doctor, the experiment is going well. Mr. B is getting ready to send a 180-volt electroshock to Mr. A."

"Are you sure we are not going too far?"

"No, we must continue."

"Are you fully aware that..."

"I have had enough! I'm done! I can't take anymore! Whatever you do next, it'll be without me!" screams Mr. B, who leaves the room determinedly.

"He took a while that one!" says Mr. A.

You have understood correctly. This test was not destined to perform a study on memory but on the degrees of submission to authority. The individual tested is not Mr. A, but Mr. B. His victim is in reality an actor who only received virtual electroshocks.

However, as we have seen with the interference of the second scientist, when two authority figures conflict, the subjugated person flees...

The test results are terrifying. 62.5% (25 out of 40) of the subjects go through with the entire experiment and inflict 450-volt electroshocks three times. They go so far as to kill their "partner", simply because they have the encouragement of an authority figure. We refer to a supreme authority to escape responsibility and thus procure a sense of impunity. The individual becomes a tool, a commanded force who does not think anymore since a more qualified person can think for him.

However, as we have seen with the interference of the second scientist, when two authority figures conflict, the subjugated person flees...

That is exactly what occurs when the advisor and the coach air out their differences. The player is dominated by a supreme authority, the advisor, who is the emblematic figure. The coach also represents an authority. If these two main actors are in conflict, the stressed child walks away from them and his goal, and adopts the evasive behavior described in 4.2 "Self-perception" in the paragraph "Doubt does not exist".

d. Code of ethics

Yet, the player himself involuntarily tries to find subtle hints of disagreement between the advisor and coach. He always goes where the information is the most reassuring for him.

The player, who is at the heart of the process, can blossom, improve, and obtain results only if the team he forms with the advisor and the coach is in perfect osmosis. Yet, the player himself involuntarily tries to find subtle hints of disagreement between the advisor and coach. He always goes where the information is the most reassuring for him.

The player often blames others for his faults because of the great stress and pressure he faces when he has to compete. He therefore looks for weaknesses in the system, and exploits them in order to "hide" himself. The player often develops this type of behavior unintentionally, but the damage is very real.

That is why the closeness and the stability of the advisor-coach relationship has proven to be difficult to obtain and guarantee in the long term. Yet, certain conditions can help avoid major pitfalls in the development of a young champion.

Work environment

The first condition for a good partnership is to clearly specify the respective roles of the advisor and the coach. Each situation is unique and the roles that I define hereunder can be allocated differently in accordance with many criteria: the presence of a parent during training or matches, the role of the parent in technical training...

It is imperative that this framework is defined unambiguously, and that it is established not according to each person's wishes, but in the best interest of the child.

It is imperative that this framework is defined unambiguously.

The advisor is the inspiration, the model. He sets the tone, the enthusiasm, and the motivation. He supervises the child and instills discipline in him. He passes on the values of the professional world by making sure that the child abides with them daily. He is often the one who "puts pressure" on the child. The advisor is the person who maintains the player's self-confidence with a daily speech.

That is why ethical rules are necessary.

The coach, on his part, passes on the technical, tactical, physical or mental tools for success, and schedules the tournaments, most of the time in partnership with the advisor. He also brings his enthusiasm and the credibility that comes from his experience.

They each respect the other's work, but since performance is a result of good overall management, there can be – and often are – opinions as to the way the other does his job.

That is why ethical rules are necessary.

Code of ethics

The relationship between the coach and the advisor must be clear and defined.

– The relationship between the coach and the advisor must be clear and defined. Who is the decision-maker (in general, the one who pays the other)? What is the coach's mission? What is expected of him? What results are expected in the short-, mid-, long-term? In other words, what is he judged on? How long does he have to prove himself?

As strange as it may seem, partnership agreements are often very vague on this subject, so much so that fired coaches do not always understand the motives behind their dismissal.

Each one knows what the other is responsible for.

– They must not infringe on each other's territory. Each one knows what the other is responsible for and must not intervene directly with the player in an area of expertise that is not their own.

This is all the more important when the number of team members increases as the player advances in the sport (agent, physical trainer, physical therapist, osteopath, sponsors, federations...). This makes each person's role even more difficult to define. That is why this principle must be applied seriously.

Each one has the right to his opinion, but this does not authorize him to discredit a team member in the eyes of the captain, the player.

– If a member disagrees with another one, he must never, under any circumstances, show it to the player because that puts the other member in a bad position. Each one has the right to his opinion, but this does not authorize him to discredit a team member in the eyes of the captain, the player. The captain must trust his team members. In case of a disagreement between two members, however, they must imperatively inform the player and the object of the disagreement must be dealt with.

– Dialogue is always the best way to settle a difference. Respecting someone means being capable of expressing your disagreement.

A team spirit

– We must always defend all of our team members in every situation despite the disagreements. If a team member is criticized or attacked, the others must defend him.

– We win together, we lose together. Losses are part of the player's training. Even if the team must intervene as little as possible, it must accept defeat, be loyal in the face of it and then, analyze the reasons for it unemotionally.

We win together, we lose together. We are loyal to each other in every situation.

– There are two moments that prove to us who our partners are: in the euphoria of great victories and in the pain of defeat. The true nature of people always reveals itself in these two circumstances. You must therefore be vigilant regarding the actions of each person in both cases.

– We help our partners: if we know some information (positive or negative) that can serve another member of the team, we must tell them. Corollary principle: we use positive speech with our partners.

Chapter 6
Frequent errors made by advisors/coaches

1. DOUBT AND ITS CONSEQUENCES

It is difficult to be an advisor. It may be even more difficult than being a coach. The advisor has the upper hand. It's due to – and thanks to – the advisor that a player develops a champion's mentality. But this great responsibility is a double-edged sword. If the advisor develops inadequate behavior, he often obtains the opposite results he expected.

If the advisor develops inadequate behavior, he often obtains the opposite results he expected.

Far from wanting to condemn them, I would like to show you the most damaging behavior of parents and coaches, and to explain their motivation and their consequences, keeping in mind that coaches are also exposed and are often not exempt from reproach.

The advisor very often lives in fear of the future. Whether he is conscious or not of the choice he has made for his child and his entire family by "gambling" everything on the career of the protégé, he nevertheless knows that there is no return ticket: it is success or nothing. It is a very exciting bet for someone who is convinced that he will lead his child to victory. However, it is a nightmare for the doubting parent!

It is a very exciting bet for someone who is convinced that he will lead his child to victory.

It is all the more difficult to handle, as we have seen before, because tennis is not a simple sport, it is a psychological sport above all. The defeats hurt. We have the feeling that we are going in the right direction, making great strides forward, and suddenly, we have to deal with a defeat we did not expect. A defeat that destroys and calls into question the certainties which were so hard to obtain through work and determination. The tennis world and the people in it are always quick to remind us of this and to press where it hurts...

It is very difficult to feel confident within this context... Very difficult for a doubting person to build trust...

Thus, different types of manifestations of doubt appear which create a climate of insecurity that is not conducive to high performance for the player.

Thus, different types of manifestations of doubt appear which create a climate of insecurity that is not conducive to high performance for the player. What we will describe hereunder describes excessive, irrational behavior and is closely linked to the incapacity of the advisor and/or coach to bear the weight of his emotions. This highly emotive behavior, of course, has repercussions on the three principal protagonists.

a. The one who questions the coach's methods

Sometimes the emotions they feel during a match make them rethink everything, including what they consider to be obtained already.

Some advisors cannot bear the emotional intensity of a match and behave negatively during and after the meets. They thus have a tendency to rethink everything, including what they consider to be obtained already.

For example, after a defeat, I have seen advisors address a coach in these terms: "She has no forehand! I thought it was better, but, in fact, it's terrible. All of this technical work amounts to nothing! She can't put the ball in the court when the game speeds up." Or: "He's not mentally strong! What's the use of training? He trains four hours a day. He plays really well during training and once there's a match... nothing!"

These remarks can be full of good sense or completely unjustified. Sometimes, it has to do with problems the player has encountered for years, even though the coach has been training him for only three months. How can we expect him to change behavior that is so deeply ingrained? In every case, it has to do with questioning the coach's capabilities, whether unintentionally or not. All these remarks implicitly accuse him of being incapable of finding solutions.

The coach slowly loses confidence in himself and in his work, and ends up passing on these doubts to the player.

In each case, this type of situation presents a deeper problem: either the coach is not communicating well with the player and/or his advisor or he is having a hard time finding the path to success.

This tug of war does have consequences: the coach loses confidence in himself and his work, and ends up passing on his doubts to the player.

The right attitude for the advisor is to talk to the coach about the problems that he would like to see settled with his child. If the coach is going through a difficult period, the advisor must let him know that he trusts and supports him in order to avoid the coach's doubts and fears being passed onto his child.

If the coach is going through a difficult period, the advisor must let him know that he trusts and supports him.

In a relationship of trust, the advisor and coach must agree on the time needed to resolve problems. The advisor must do his best to see if a real improvement is happening gradually every day or if they are hitting a wall. During losses, it is important to never speak emotionally in the heat of the moment. Having taken the time to reflect, he must regroup and ask the coach to share observations, his feelings about the evolution of the situation and the solutions he wants to put in place.

b. The one who judges his opponent

Another fault that reveals a doubt in the advisor or the coach and shows fear of the future consists of sizing up the level of the child's opponent before the match. Fear of the unknown leads parents to search for reference points.

Thus, in the relatively closed world of high-level tennis, all the players know each other and have played each other. Each player has his own idea about his opponent's game. Moreover, the ranking system allows the players to gauge themselves. It is easy to step onto the court with a good idea of what the opponent is worth.

Judgment is the enemy of performance.

Judgment is the enemy of performance because it directly influences behavior during matches. Rather than play your game without questioning yourself, you play "not to lose" when the opponent is judged to be weaker or "to get a good score" when he is judged to be stronger. In both cases, you are headed straight for defeat.

The advisors and coaches are often the first to judge their child's opponents. "Ah, you are playing so-and-so. It is a good round. You should take advantage of it..." How can we then expect the players to be relaxed and focused on what they have to do? It is difficult when we do not give ourselves the right to lose. They also know how to pass on their fear or admiration for an opponent: "It will be hard in the next round... Hold on anyway. It is already great to have made it this far." The outcome of the match is already decided in advance.

c. The one who thinks small

Some advisors or some coaches, for fear of being disappointed or of putting too much pressure on the player, have a tendency to think small. They set small goals and sometimes set them even lower. They do not invest the necessary funds so that the player can work in acceptable conditions. They see themselves as small, so they also see their player that way.

Unfortunately, we always end up resembling the image we make of ourselves, so when the image is small, there are few chances that the result will be great!

In reality, they send a clear message to the player: "I do not think that you are capable, so I set goals according to your capacities" or, "Given your chances, it is unreasonable to take such an important financial risk".

Sometimes the advisor and/or coach unintentionally send this type of message to the player: "I don't think that you're capable, so I set goals according to your capacities".

d. The one who changes his mind

Some advisors change their minds or direction too often. Each defeat calls everything into question.

The match gives clear indications on the path to take to succeed and when we have seen a dozen matches, the key elements we need to concentrate on are already identified. The direction to take during training has been decided and put into place.

Yet, some advisors constantly question these choices and systematically demand that the work be centered on what posed a problem during the match. The player and the coach therefore find themselves in a terribly unstable situation and do not have enough time to get to the heart of problems and achieve tangible progress.

e. The one who gives too much information

Stress is at its highest pitch for everyone when a match approaches: for the player, of course, but also for the advisor, who suffers with his child, and for the coach, who puts his work on the line during each match. Has the child improved? Has he integrated the points they have worked on? Will the advisor

The player needs a simple and clear battle plan before the match.

or coach be able to find the right words at critical moments? The player needs a simple and clear battle plan before the match. He needs the coach and advisor to give him confidence.

One problem is that the coach and/or advisor often feel even greater apprehension than the player himself. Confined to a much more passive role during the match, they await the judgment (victory or defeat), conscious of the consequences of either outcome.

Let the child make mistakes. That is how he will learn. By avoiding errors, you are preventing him from improving, learning and having self-confidence.

Faced with this stress, the advisors and coaches often give too much information: what to do tactically, technically, what to think about, what to do in one situation, what to do in another... So much so that the player is completely disoriented when he steps onto the court.

This behavior once again reveals the lack of confidence in the player and in his capacity to find solutions to the problems he will face. The advisor and the coach must trust the player, give him a simple and clear battle plan, let him make mistakes and find solutions.

f. The one who cannot accept defeat

I have seen the most horrendous behavior after a defeat. Yes, I know how difficult it is to see your child fight and suffer, but I also know how hard they fight and the investment they put in. I know how much they give of themselves, and the advisor must respect this and act in the best interest of the player.

Yet, in the face of defeat, it is unfortunately usual to see verbally or physically violent behavior on the part of advisors or coaches. In their eyes, it is a response to what they have experienced as an aggression. Unable to handle the pressure of the match and the negative emotions they feel, they "take revenge" by freeing all of the violence accumulated during those few hours. During what we incorrectly call the match debriefing (which I would qualify more as a death sentence), the advisor and/or the coach enumerate all the deplorable errors committed by the player, go on about his incapacity to win, his lack of mental strength...

These individuals do not understand that a tennis match is not a mathematical equation. They just cannot accept defeat, and will even go so far as to punish a player.

In all of these cases, the advisor and/or the coach gives a very negative connotation to the match. The player will develop a growing anxiety: "If I lose this match, I will be subjected to violence." Once again, his performance will be altered in the future.

If such behavior from parents is reprehensible, it is unacceptable in the coach, whose only objective is to lead his protégé to victory. The 7 commandments of a coach illustrate the attitude to adopt after matches. See chapter 4.6.

2. HOW THE ADVISOR FORMS THE PLAYER'S ATTITUDE

In his approach to education, the advisor must be conscious that he ingrains "internal ways of functioning" in his child. The player often unconsciously reproduces some of these attitudes.

Inadequate behavior on the part of a player during a match is often the reproduction of the advisor's behavior off the court.

The tennis court perfectly reveals the true nature of a human being. To an informed observer, what happens during a match teaches more about the personality of the team members than the hundreds of hours spent off the court.

a. How the advisor creates the player's attitude

I meet all types of parents in the tennis world. One of my

player's fathers has developed the bad habit of lashing out at everyone. He lives in constant conflict. It is apparently his way of exorcizing the daily stress and anxiety he feels about the future. He does not excuse any error made by his son's entourage. He chooses a scapegoat and develops a conflictual relationship with him up until it gets to a breaking point. Then, he starts all over again with someone else.

In reality, this player reproduces the behavior that has been handed down by his father.

His son has a lot of potential. He is gifted with exceptional physical skills and a very powerful right-hand. Despite this, he invariably makes mistakes during matches. He gives the impression that he is hitting shots by accident and with a lot of violence. The greater the emotional intensity of the match, the more he hits blindly and commits a series of unforced errors. In key moments of the match, he hits even more violently, instead of making his opponent play and cooling off the rally. He ends up losing control of the match. Every coach who trains him in the future will be surprised by his way of doing things, and will remain perplexed in regards to his attitude.

In reality, this player reproduces the behavior that has been handed down by his father. Like him, he was "programmed" to experience the pressure in a negative way. He reacts by hitting any which way, and not by dealing with the problems.

Of course, neither one is conscious of this mimicry.

b. The player who gets enraged during a match

When I started working with a father and daughter, I quickly understood that they formed a united couple. The player was young, but highly performing. She was a great competitor. She was very aggressive and could hit extraordinarily well. However, during matches, she would get excessively frustrated once things were not going as planned. She became enraged, leading her to systematically lose confidence in her game, to question her skills, and to become negative. And of course, unforced errors started to pile up.

I asked to attend some training sessions with her father, who was a charming, very motivated and hard-working man. The first training sessions ran smoothly, but I knew that they were making an effort to present themselves in the best light. I had to find a way to observe them in unfavorable conditions, when the player was overcome with fatigue, or having a bad day.

So, I found a way to attend the training sessions "at-distance", and I ended up finding what I was looking for. The advisor was becoming enraged the moment his daughter was unable to follow his directions. He asked her to play a succession of three shots in one area, then three in another. When she was unable to do it, he became irritated and verbally violent. I explained to him that his daughter was just repeating a situation she had experienced thousands of times. It was ingrained in her: failure automatically created anger and frustration.

Yet, the father did not seem to understand his daughter's attitude and showed his impatience. I asked him: "How do you expect your daughter to control herself when you're incapable of doing it yourself? How do you expect her to behave differently to what you've shown her daily since she was four years old?" My words could not resolve the problem, but at least they had the merit of being clear. If he wanted her behavior to change, he first had to show her how.

If he wanted her behavior to change, he first had to show her how.

c. The player who prefers to trail in order to react

Another type of behavior that I often see at matches is that of a player who never acts but who reacts. Some players take the reins and start a match full speed ahead. They take immediate and radical initiatives, and they often have trouble keeping up the same rhythm throughout the match. These players have a tendency to run out of breath during the match, to lose intensity and when their opponent catches up to them, end up collapsing from exhaustion.

Many other players approach a match indifferently. They suffer and only react once they are trailing. They only act when defeat becomes a real possibility. In general, the parents of these players behave the same way in life. They find it very difficult to make decisions and often refer to others. However, when they feel threatened, they react violently.

All of these behaviors, which were reproduced by the children on the court, were ingrained in them at a very young age. It is one of the perversions of what I call "programming". The parents unconsciously serve as their models and the children reproduce the same type of behavior when faced with the same stimulus.

We can foresee a certain number of these behaviors by pointing them out beforehand. It is sometimes necessary to change the behavior of the advisors so that the children can learn to have winning reactions.

Chapter 7
My personal experiences

1. A NEWCOMER LOST IN A WORLD OF INSIDERS

The majority of athletic stories I have witnessed within my Academy these past ten years have concerned children who were not educated as champions. That is the case with the majority of children. They are held to a level of excellence in tennis, but they are not given the handbook for it, mainly because, most parents do not have it. They made the choice to go into tennis as they would have chosen any other domain. They are often powerless because they do not have the answers to the questions before them. When I go to Grand Slams, in the players areas, and check out this little world, I sympathize with the parents and the players. They are not insiders, they ignore the traditions and customs of this world, they do not have the keys to success, and they do not understand the business. In brief, they are ideal prey for the sharks that know this world all too well...

Tennis parents are not insiders. They are ideal prey for the sharks that know this world all too well...

2. HOW TO CHOOSE AN AGENT?

The choice of an agent for your child is extremely important in the evolution of his career. It is a heavy responsibility that weighs on the shoulders of parents. And they do not really have the competence and necessary wisdom to make the right decisions.

The first step for them must consist of understanding the rules of the game: financial, legal, and social. They must learn how strategic decisions are made in the tennis world: why an equipment supplier signs a contract with a player, and what he expects of the player in exchange. Some agents consider the player to be a partner in the learning process, others make outrageous promises devoid of any economic reality, and the parents often go along because they do not know any better.

The second step for the parents involves finding an agent who they feel they can trust, who knows how to listen and who understands their specific problems. The player must land very good contracts when everything is going well, but also must have a minimum of material comfort and good work conditions during difficult times.

The agent must above all be a trustworthy, honest person who gives good advice and is a great marketer.

The player and his family are his partners. They set the goals together and the agent constantly informs them of the strategies he puts in place to attain them. The agent must guarantee the financial durability of the player's business. Like the head of the family, he makes the player independent and adult enough to fructify his capital, keeping in mind the number of legal, financial and social constraints involved.

The agent must guarantee the financial durability of the player's business.

3. MY PERSONAL EXPERIENCES

When I opened my Academy ten years ago, I did not know where to find the keys to knowing how to win at a very professional level. Therefore, I relied more on talent than on a state of mind. The education of the players is already done, and it is up to us to find the solutions, to show them the path to victory.

We find many different cases in the stories I will evoke. Once success occurs, it is often because the main elements of my method were put in place. The three main team members (the player, the advisor and the coach) have found their rightful place and are confronted with many situations.

Beyond their unique nature, all of these stories shed a particular light on the way we reach or do not reach a very high level.

MARCOS BAGHDATIS

Marcos Baghdatis has just written a book about his extraordinary story, that of a little Cypriot who became an Adidas icon. It is a book that illustrates all the complexities of a champion's life. Marcos wrote it without resentment, without wanting to settle scores; but at the heart of it, we perceive a need to understand. For despite his big heart and his wide smile, Marcos has hidden deep wounds since being taken from the sweetness of his native island as a teenager.

Marcos has hidden deep wounds since being taken from the sweetness of his native island as a teenager.

At a very young age he was subjected, by proxy, to his father's dream of having a tennis champion in his family. His older brother, Marinos, long held that role until the day he was a victim of a terrible car accident that left him in a coma for many months. The family lost its bearings when faced with the sudden tragedy of this eldest son who had so much potential. His mother wept constantly. His father barely uttered a word. And Marcos, too young to truly understand the situation, felt completely abandoned by this brother who was a hero to him. The coach who was training him left the island, so Marcos found himself even more alone. Marcos no longer touched a racket, and started hanging out outside all day with a bunch of friends.

The story threatened to end there. But one day, on a whim, he went to his mother and declared: "Mom, stop crying. I'll do it. I'll play tennis and I'll beat all of them." With this cry of

"Mom, stop crying. I'll do it. I'll play tennis and I'll beat all of them."

love, he wanted to show that he had had enough of all the pain and that he wanted life to be as it was before.

He then begged his father to give him a chance at tennis. The story began in a whirlwind of emotions within a child who wanted to both ease his mother's pain and satisfy the dreams of his strict, but loving father. His father had not given up on his dream and he spurred this change in Marcos, even though the young boy was much more passionate about soccer. "My father had done everything to have a champion in the family," recounts Marcos. "I had no choice. It had to be done. When he trained me in Cyprus, I never stopped talking about my passion for tennis. But he didn't realize that there was something else behind it. Even today, I think he's convinced that I wanted to play tennis... But I still don't know why I said I wanted to. I just never said no."

Even today, I think he is convinced that I wanted to play tennis...

At thirteen, Marcos became the No.1 Cypriot player. He made the Davis Cup team and traveled to Europe for international tournaments in the under-14 category. That is when I discovered him at the Petits As tournament. I invited him to the Academy in Montreuil to take a test in October 1999. The test was conclusive. His arrival at the Academy was scheduled for February. This would leave him time to compete in the Davis Cup match against Uganda. Little Marcos was completely oblivious of the stakes involved and the nightmare began. It started precisely on the plane that brought him to France on Sunday, February 13th, accompanied by his silent father. In a Montreuil hotel, they met his future coach, Jean-Paul Damit, who instantly had very high expectations for him. "With me, you'll never make the same mistake twice." He woke up in tears the next morning at 7:30 am, next to his father, who was still mute. Then he came to the Academy to train.

The afternoon session was a catastrophe, to Jean-Paul's displeasure. I arrived to sign the contract but Marcos ran away crying... then came back to sign it. Everything was done very quickly. Marcos felt terribly abandoned, since he had not received a thorough explanation about what was going on. His father unintentionally saved him by telling him: "This is a one-way ticket." He did not leave his son a choice, and did not have an easy solution at his disposal. Marcos' tears continued to flow throughout the first two weeks. I lacked experience and was unable to help one of my first pupils. I called his father. "You know, your son cries a lot..."

I called his father. "You know, your son cries a lot..."

"Don't worry, it will pass," he replied.

He was right. He was intelligent and sufficiently sharp to know that if he left an opening, if he let his emotions take over, the beautiful dream would crumble. He was right. When we decided something, we had to eliminate any alternatives one by one.

In the meantime, Marcos walked around like a zombie. He did not want to do anything and dreamt of Cyprus day and night. He went home for the first time after four months, just for a few days. The following year, he did not see his mother for ten months. Traumatized by these brief and painful journeys home, he preferred not to return to visit. Thanks to his host family, the Benhaïms, he found comfort and balance after all the work which was also done as a family in the Academy.

Traumatized by these brief and painful journeys home, he preferred to not return to visit.

The tension between Marcos and his father got worse due to their separation and lack of mutual understanding.

On my end, I began to spend more and more time with Marcos. Since the host family, initially located in Montreuil, moved, I picked him up every morning to bring him to the Academy: a two-hour daily trip, during which we got to know and like one another. We talked about everything, and I realized that his trust in me was growing every day. At the same time, he felt a lot of pressure from me. He knew I believed in him and he did not want to disappoint me. On my end, I insisted on the things that seemed important and I pushed him further. He found a remarkable coach in Jean-Paul Damit, a coach who asked a lot of him, but who could also let go when the need arose. He taught him life lessons, but also took the time to listen. I know today that Marcos is aware of how important Jean-Paul was in his progress...

"I missed my parents so much that the idea of disappointing them was even more unbearable than the separation."

We quickly sensed a burning desire in him to succeed. At 14 and a half years old, already very mature for a young teenager, Marcos realized that he was alone and that the only way to survive the situation was to accept what was happening to him. He understood that he could not turn back the clock. He had to live up to his family's expectations; and his father's in particular. In his book, he says: "I missed my parents so much that the idea of disappointing them was even more unbearable than the separation."

When an obstacle stood in his way, he crushed it with all the maturity he had despite his tender age.

One thing was clear, though. He no longer accepted his father dictating what he had to do from distance. His father was no longer involved and had thus lost all legitimacy. Marcos made him pay for what he considered to be abandonment. "You are no longer here. You have no rights. You wanted to leave me, now deal with it." Whenever his father told him something over the telephone, Marcos became defensive. They only saw each other one week a year. And one day, it reached a breaking-point. Marcos told his father: "I don't want to speak to you anymore." Their relationship seemed to have reached a point of no return. His father, being a Mediterranean, did not take it lightly. He screamed reproach down the telephone:

"Can you believe it? It's the first time my son doesn't want to speak to me!" That period was tense. Marcos had just won the world junior title before joining the professional ranks. It was at that moment that everything started happening. But he was handicapped with a groin injury and his emotions swung between anxiety about failure and stress about losing his form. His father became more and more anxious. I listened, I had hindsight, and at the same time, I was responsible for him. I therefore told his father: "Christos, your son is full of doubt. It's worrisome because he's at a point where he's going to find out whether he'll succeed or not. It's the moment of truth. He's no longer in the juniors. We're playing for real now. We're dealing the cards. Your son's worried. He's injured and is having doubts. You're his father. You must act like a father and reassure him, instead of adding to his stress. So forget your worries, call him and give him some confidence." Marcos' father listened to my advice and made up with his son.

"You're his father. You must act like a father and reassure him instead of giving him more stress."

I think that this was a turning point in their relationship because it was at that moment that his father truly understood his role.

So I decided to make him more independent, to help him mature into an adult who was capable of making his own decisions, and taking his fate into his own hands, which he had already started doing. He was unhappy with his physical trainer and came to see me to voice his complaints. So I told him: "I understand, Marcos. You have the right to think what you do. You have to go see him and tell him. If you must separate from him, I'll support your decision, but you have to explain it to him." It was at that moment that Marcos understood that his destiny was in his own hands. I would accompany him, would always be there to support or advise him, but I wanted him to realize that he was master of his decisions and therefore of his future.

"Marcos, you need Guillaume, not any other coach. Guillaume will be your coach!"

When he separated from Jean-Paul, he came to see me: "What do we do now? You can replace him with whoever you want, except Guillaume (Peyre)."

"Marcos, you need Guillaume, not any other coach. Guillaume will be your coach!"

I knew why he did not want this coach, who happened to be the best in the Academy: Guillaume had the reputation of being very strict and Marcos did not want to lose the freedom that he had just started to taste. He worked very hard with Guillaume, and Guillaume let him keep his freedom in return. With 120 matches and very convincing victories against Canas and Vinciguerra, he rolled through his first year on the circuit like a marathon runner and ranked No.190 in the world with the world junior championship title on top of that.

Then the groin injury halted his progress for four months.

At the beginning of the year, Guillaume toughened up the sessions with a firm desire to make Marcos lose the weight he had gained during his injury period. But he hurried things at a time when Marcos, injured, had to start from scratch after a long lay-off. Their relationship turned sour very quickly. During a tournament in the Czech Republic in April, they clashed. Marcos was convinced that he was the only one who knew what he should do.

His hand started to lose all feeling. He risked paralysis.

After the break with Guillaume, I tried to ease the tensions. "No problem, Marcos, we'll find an answer..." In the meantime, I trained him during the French Open qualification rounds where he was eliminated in the last round following a bad match against Marc Gicquel. Then, he started over with an Academy coach with whom it did not work out. I trained him again in October and he soon won a tournament, his first $25,000, then a $125,000 by beating Dominik Hrbaty, No.14 in the world, in the final. Marcos, No.250 at the time, found himself on the threshold of the Top 100. Then came the big preparation for the Australian Open. He got through the qualifications then reached the last-sixteen by beating notably Ljubicic and Robredo, before losing to Roger Federer. Alas, he was once again sidelined with another injury. A nerve in his right forearm was causing problems and his hand started to lose all feeling. He risked paralysis. A little taken aback, the doctors we consulted during the Australian Open diagnosed epicondylitis – tennis elbow!

But Gilles Daubinet, a trauma doctor with whom I work, discovered the root of the problem. At nine o'clock at night (!), he found the nature of the injury – a compressed nerve – and called one of the best French hand surgeons, Dr. Le Viet, to perform an emergency operation three days later. This is a threatening and dangerous operation for a tennis player. The surgeon must intervene very close to the hand and cut the nerves. The player must wait for the muscle to knit back together... and especially hope that the arm completely regains feeling.

Marcos was very courageous. But he became depressed immediately after the operation.

He had been turning around in circles for months. He knew that he needed a full-time coach. I was unable to give him what he wanted from me. I had to take care of my family and I refused to leave them alone, without me. He needed me? No problem, I could give him my time. But, I could not agree to travel around the world with him all year round, leaving my wife and very young children behind. After the 2005 US Open, he was at the end of his tether. We were in the "players' lounge", near the sofas. He was sitting on the floor. He wanted to talk but did not know how to go about it. I sat down next to him.

"Patrick, I don't feel the present situation is good for me now."

"I know. I can see you're not progressing. Marcos, I've always told you I'll train you if that's the best solution. If that's no longer the case in the future, we'll change things. It's not a problem for me. I want the best for you! I believe so much in you that I want to offer you the best conditions."

"I feel I need someone with me full-time. I get very bored on the circuit. I feel alone, so I mull things over. I ask myself thousands of questions and I lose confidence in myself. When you're with me, it's perfect; but will you continue? Are you prepared to travel all year with me?"

"I'd like to work with Guillaume (Peyre) again. I know him well, he knows me well and I trust him."

"Marcos, we've had this conversation many times. I'll do everything I can to help but within certain limits. To train you, make some trips with you, like for Grand Slams, sure, but I can't do more than that."

"Then I think it best we find someone for me. The present solution doesn't suit me."

"No problem, Marcos. Have you thought about someone you'd feel good with?"

"If you can't be that person, Patrick, then I have thought of someone. I'd like to work with Guillaume (Peyre) again. I know him well, he knows me well and I trust him."

"Guillaume's currently training another player at the Academy; but you're my priority, so I'll find a way for him to train you once we return to Paris."

"Thanks, Patrick."

I did not manage my post-partnership with Marcos correctly. In hindsight, I understand today that our emotional bond was too strong and that it interfered with our work. Too much passion alters how you contemplate situations.

Anyway, let us not beat around the bush. I made a promise to myself when I stopped training Marcos full-time: "Whatever your feelings, you must show him that nothing has changed between us, that you believe in him and that you'll invest in him exactly like before. In reality, I'm suffering too. Marcos is a bit like my son. I've spent more time with him than with anyone else these last few years. In 2005, we shared so many emotions, from tears to the euphoria of victory, and depression. I've shared his life like a father, a brother, a friend, a confidante. It's difficult when it ends suddenly, but deep down inside of me, I know that this is the best solution. I know that I must make the decision but it's hard!"

So I accepted being "far away", but not too far. I did not want to let him go. And there was that day when I tried to rouse him: "Marcos, it has been a while since you've not given it your all. You're close to your goal. You're in the Top 100. You must make a living, you must get moving. Your parents and I have done everything to help you get here. Now you must do it yourself. This is no time for self-pity!" This was no longer the coach talking, even if I tried to ignore it. I was talking with my feelings. They were also, clumsily, the words of someone who wanted to keep Marcos close to him.

And there was that day when I tried to rouse him. It was no longer the coach talking, even if I tried to ignore that fact.

But for Marcos, it was like a turning-point. He felt like an adult as of that day. He would now take his fate completely into his own hands. He wanted me at his side, but not like a substitute father. As for me, I wanted him to remain my Marcos, the one who asked me what he should do after training sessions, the one who called me from the United States to know if he should train once or twice. No. Marcos had grown up. He finally knew himself and knew what it would take to get to the top.

Marcos needed space, and I had to understand that it was not calling into question the sincerity and the depth of our relationship. He had simply become an adult.

Our relationship was very tense over the six months that followed. We both suffered.

I love you sincerely, like a son. You are a great champion and, above all, you are a great man.

I am happy that we have now found a balance in our relationship. Marcos, I know that you know that. I love you sincerely, like a son and a friend, and I can never thank you enough for what you have given me on a personal and professional level. You are a great champion and, above all, you are a great man.

Marcos reached the Australian Open final against Roger Federer in January 2006. In July, he lost only in the semi-final at Wimbledon against Rafael Nadal, while reaching the best ranking of his blossoming career: No.8 in the world.

Like those people who suddenly find themselves thrown onto the world stage, Marcos is surrounded by a lot of people but he is also terribly alone, not knowing if people are around him for him or because they have something to gain. Like all champions, he knows who he is, but he also needs a sincere and professional external viewpoint. He knows that he will always find that with me.

For Marcos' future, I want to create a team, a "Team Baghdatis", which will bring to his side the specialists he needs in order to aim for the top of the world rankings.

ARAVANE REZAI

I met Aravane Rezai at the 2006 US Open. I was impressed by the quality of her shots. I spent time with her and her brother, Anouch, who is both her sparring partner and coach. We get along well. She had a very good tournament and reached the last-sixteen. I met her parents on my return to Paris and notably, the famous and very controversial, Arsalan Rezai. This first meeting was peculiar. Arsalan was very courteous, but he took me aback: "We made it here together as a family and we'll finish together as a family. We don't need anything. Thank you very much." The message was clear.

Yet I know, after having spent some time with Aravane and Anouch that they needed some support. But they did not trust anyone and did not want to owe anything to anybody.

But they did not trust anyone and did not want to owe anything to anybody.

However, I stayed in contact and every time an opportunity presented itself, I spoke to Mr. Rezai on the phone. We started to get to know one another. We put in place an outline for a partnership at the French Open; he wanted, like me, to supervise his daughter during the tournament. Then came Wimbledon, where we spent ten days together in the same house. It was then, living with them, that I started to really get to know them, to like them and to understand how they work.

They told me their very unique and touching story.

Mr. and Mrs. Rezai left their native country, Iran, to try their luck in France. They did not have any money. He was an automobile mechanic and she made dresses at home. When Mr. Rezai watched Yannick Noah's victory at the French Open, he was deeply moved. So much emotion, the beauty of the sport, and on top of that, it was shared as a family! Yannick leapt into his father's arms at the end of the match.

So much emotion, the beauty of the sport, and on top of that, it was shared as a family!

So they play outside, in the middle of winter, without lighting.

At that very moment, he decided to launch himself into this adventure with his children. He began training them alone, without any means. He did not even have the money to rent a tennis court for the day! So they played outside, in the middle of winter, without lighting. Mr. Rezai brought along a coal stove to provide some heat on the court. For lighting, he parked his car in front of the court and left the headlamps on.

Aravane was promising. When she reached the age to take part in professional tournaments, they needed to travel. He drove all across Europe in their van, which also served as dining-room and bedroom. They had to be self-sufficient and made do with what they had! Mr. Rezai supported his children in this lifetime project. He gave them the desire to make it. Their working conditions strengthened their determination. They had a good understanding of the true value of money. Mr. Rezai insisted that they participate in all discussions, even negotiations. He continued to train them, to teach them how to make it in life.

In my opinion, what they have accomplished with their means is quite simply remarkable.

In order to understand this family, you must know who they are, where they have come from, what they went through and how they felt. Their way of working becomes easier to comprehend that way. In my opinion, what they have accomplished with little or no means is quite simply remarkable. I also believe that Mr. Rezai possesses extraordinary qualities without which he would never have been able to take his daughter to such a level.

Contrary to the image some people sometimes have of him, he is very intelligent and shrewd. His excessive behavior can be explained by the uniqueness of their story; which, of course, does not justify that behavior. Aravane has extraordinary potential that is just waiting to be realized. She is currently ranked No.50 in the WTA rankings and her progress margin is enormous. Right now, the focus needs to be on getting her into the Top 10.

I am lucky that the Rezai family trusts me. Our partnership is very constructive. It exists to help each person find his or her most effective role.

Mr. Rezai is the head of the family, the one who exudes energy and makes the major decisions. Mrs. Rezai brings balance and love. She is extremely devoted and generous. Anouch works hard and is interested in many things. He trains hard so that he can put his qualities at his sister's service. He is open-minded and motivated to improve.

This family balance is the cement of success. It must be conserved by any means necessary. As for me, I advise them and together we reflect on Aravane's future. She can still make formidable progress in many fields. For this to happen, the family must call on the skills of specialists, and I have gradually put together a team that is united in fulfilling their needs.

I have gradually put together a team that is united in fulfilling their needs.

VALENTINE FAUVIAU

The story of Valentine Fauviau illustrates the difficulties that can face a player when she suddenly loses her advisor, also discovering that he had never totally believed in her.

In Valentine's case, the circumstances surrounding the loss of her main partner were drastic and her fall brutal. Suddenly suffocated and void of all hope, Valentine was unable to overcome such a dramatic turn of events. She had lost the person who had programmed her and accompanied her on her road to success.

She saw a man go to jail – her own father – charged with drugging the opponents of her and her brother in order to weaken them. A man whose dastardly scheme evolved into second-degree murder when a young man's life was tragically ended at the wheel of his car in a ditch.

In one fell swoop, the career of Valentine Fauviau, France's top tennis hope, stopped dead.

Plunged into total family crisis, what must the young Valentine have thought when faced with the knowledge of such astonishing deeds? That some of her wins were fixed and thus undeserved? That her advisor believed so little in her that he was reduced to go to such extremes? In one fell swoop, the career of Valentine Fauviau, France's top tennis hope, stopped dead. And yet, she was an exceptional player.

From the age of 8, her athletic qualities enabled her to hurl herself into her serves while looking entirely relaxed. She played with such suppleness and ease. She was a fighter who gave everything to her sport.

For before stooping to such unimaginably extreme acts, Christophe Fauviau had managed to develop his daughter's skills by putting her under intense pressure, which is considered normal behavior in the demanding world of tennis. He could be very hard on her, bursting into her bedroom at four in the morning to send her out jogging. Again, nothing unusual from people who want results. Valentine never questioned him and complied.

The world of tennis marketing wasted no time in offering her financial deals.

At 12 years old, she was ranked 1/6. For her age, she was the highest ranked girl in France, probably one of the highest in the world. The world of tennis marketing wasted no time in offering her financial deals.

At the time, her father was in an ongoing dispute with her League regarding its objectives: a classic and customary case of incomprehension on the part those who want the system to do everything for their child. Like many tennis parents, he failed to see why the League refused to meet all his demands. For such parents, not doing the maximum for their child displays a lack of belief. And Christophe Fauviau needed this belief. Filled with doubt and anxiety about the future, he needed the League's outside help. Because if the League decided to do everything for Valentine, it would mean recognition of her as a very strong player, and this would reassure Christophe. But the League would not yield, resulting in conflict. While looking for a landing-pad for Valentine, he showed an interest in my Academy. During our first meetings, I detected no difference from other tennis parents. I'd seen hundreds just like him, some even more extreme in their approach. When I was told about the tragedy, other names sprang to mind well before I learned it was him.

Unbeknown to everyone, he had descended into total paranoia which drove him to finally commit crime. He had created a world that revolved around his daughter, made up of good guys and bad guys. The good guys were those who believed in Valentine, the bad guys all the rest. Finally, he saw only enemies all around. He worked with mediocre coaches and got angry with one of them over a nasty problem of expenses. He ended up convinced that the entire world was out to get him, that the fight for survival was only possible through uniting his family against the rest of the world.

Every morning, he would barge into my office telling me: "I didn't sleep all night."

I can understand his logic even if I do not share it. Of course, we work in an environment that shows no mercy, but we must put things into perspective. He only saw the negative. Every morning, he would barge into my office telling me: "I didn't sleep all night". I know how the quest for perfection can be an exhausting battle, but Christophe Fauviau got carried away...

"No one else can help me. Only you can!", she told me at the end of our conversation.

Until the day he was arrested stepping off the train in Dax, in front of his shocked daughter. At that time, I did not really know Valentine. But the day her father was sent to prison, she called me to outline what had happened. "No one else can help me. Only you!" she told me at the end of our conversation.

Our contact had been very limited, but she was convinced that I was the only person who could step into the role of advisor. Her survival instincts dictated this attitude. She was unconsciously seeking to recreate the same environment, the one that had always been favorable to her. In that cruel moment, Valentine told herself that the only way to make it was to find someone who could achieve the same things with her that her father did. And there was only one advisor in her environment with the same strong belief in this logic of high performance: me. She felt that I was that person. Breaking off my vacation, I took her home for a year and took her under my wing.

As she was very distressed, I listened to her a lot, thinking that she would free herself from all of her demons. By doing so, I was undoubtedly keeping her in a state of analysis instead of trying to get her to act. We needed to leave the psychologist's couch to get back onto the court. I should have been more assertive with her: "You've been through a very difficult experience. Get everything out of your system now and afterwards you'll get down to work, instead of complaining to everyone."

Having received my compassion, she continued to heap pity on herself. She was unable to reform an ideal. I could see that she was deteriorating and that we could not control the situation, so I tried to take the bull by the horns. The more time passed, the more I felt that my motivation outdid hers. She had a unique opportunity to take over her father's project, to use her exceptional talent in order to shine. Instead of this, I watched her become less and less motivated every day.

Certainly, the absence of her father, the advisor for whom she would give everything, weighed on her and demotivated her. But more than that, it was what he had done that really affected Valentine. Drugging her opponents was tantamount to telling her that he did not truly believe in her abilities. It showed that he had reservations about her talent and doubted the future.

So what had always seemed natural for Valentine, reaching the very top, suddenly seemed unattainable. That was why, after trying for two years and not seeing any future, I decided to tell her mother that it was for the best that Valentine return to school.

So what had always seemed natural for Valentine, reaching the very top, suddenly seemed unattainable.

Valentine maintains that she has not abandoned the idea of becoming a tennis champion, but she has stagnated since leaving the Academy... She has been gradually rebuilding herself over the past two years.

Despite what she has gone through, I believe in Valentine. I think that she is a young girl with a great deal of skill. I also believe that she still has the means to succeed in life. I have confidence in her capabilities and I have no doubt that she will be able to bounce back in tennis or elsewhere...

I also believe that she still has the means to succeed in life.

JULIA VAKULENKO

Julia had a very special childhood. She was born in Yalta, Ukraine. After her parents separated, she moved to Belgrade, Serbia, at the age of seven. Her mother had fallen in love with a man who lived in that city. Gifted at tennis, she dived passionately into the sport and became the Serbian under-14 champion.

That was when her mother separated from her second husband, with whom she had a son.

The first seven years of her life in Ukraine, the next seven in Serbia, then seven years in Spain, and now she is at the Academy.

Convinced that Spain was the best place for her daughter to pursue her tennis dreams, her mother decided to move to Barcelona. Julia began playing in professional tournaments and had some very good results. In 2005, she reached the very respectable position of No.70 in the world, but her average ranking was between No.100 and No.120. After some difficult events in her private life, she suffered a first nervous breakdown in 2005, which lasted six months, then a second in 2006, which also lasted six months, coupled with a bout of anorexia.

She was full of hope. She had nothing: no money, no coach, no structure.

In November 2006, on the advice of a friend, she came to the Academy. I still clearly remember the day we sat down in my office to discuss her future. I had just finished working with her for a week, to get an idea of her potential. She was full of hope. She had nothing: no money, no coach, no structure.

"I feel good at the Academy. I'd like to stay if possible. I'd like you to train me if you can."

"Julia, as you know, I don't have a lot of spots available. I don't want be wrong about a player's potential. You're 23 years old, you're ranked No.120...I have to get a sense of your potential. What are your goals?"

"I know I have untapped potential. I've suffered a lot in my life. I'm not interested in playing tennis unless I can excel in it. If not, I'd rather stop altogether and raise a family. I truly believe I can do great things. That's why I keep on going."

"Tell me more. What great things do you believe you can accomplish?"

"I want to compete in the Masters Cup at the end of the year."

"You have to be in the Top 8 to do that! You know that, don't you?"

"Yes, I know, but I think I can do it."

"All right. I like your goals. Now, I just need to know if I think they're achievable. I'm leaving for Miami tomorrow for three weeks to attend the Orange Bowl with a group of players from the Academy who are participating in the tournament. You're coming with me. We'll do a test. At the end of the test, I'll know if I sufficiently believe in your potential or not."

"I want to compete in the Masters Cup at the end of the year. I think I can do it." Spoken by Julia Vakulenko, ranked No.120 in the world at the time.

"Great."

The moment is etched in my memory. She had seemed very subdued, very unsure of herself. But in spite of this, I had felt great strength in her. When I opened a door for her, her face suddenly lit up. It felt like I was offering her the future she was waiting for. I truly had the feeling that I was relighting a lamp that had been out for too long.

She accompanied me to Miami. I brought along one of the physical trainers from the Academy. We worked very hard. She had not done any sports for six months due to her depression, so we had to start from scratch. Her body was flabby and lacking in muscle. She suffered but she hung on. She rebuilt herself every day and the level of her game continued to rise during training. Despite fatigue, she was extremely focused, and even if she broke down in tears at times during training, I pretended not to notice and we kept on working. She ended up pulling herself together and gave even more in the sessions.

Even if she broke down in tears at times during training, I pretended not to notice and we kept on working. She ended up pulling herself together and gave even more in the sessions.

I was confident. At the end of December, I officially told her that I had agreed to work with her. What she had shown me definitely convinced me that she had unquestionable potential. Her physical transformation was plain to see. Her confidence had returned. She was ready. Two months later, she qualified for the Australian Open and won her first-round match. Then she reached No.50 in the world, securing good results right through to May when she participated in two tournaments. In the first, she beat Kim Clijsters, No.6 in the world, who decided

Julia rose to No.33 in the world following her victories over Mauresmo, Clijsters and Safina.

to put an end to her career after that match. In the second, she reached the semi-final, beating Amélie Mauresmo, No.3 in the world, along the way, and Dinara Safina, No.10. Julia had risen to No.33 in the world.

JAN SILVA

Jan Silva is a young American who was only four years old when I met him. Scott, his father, was a former professional African-American basketball player who works in social services in Sacramento. His mother, Mari Määttänen, who is Finnish, was a tennis club coach. When Jan was born, his mother took him to tennis courts in his bassinet while she gave lessons.

Jan is the living incarnation of my method on how to educate children.

Jan is the living incarnation of my method on how to educate children, even if his case is unique since he was not intentionally programmed. His father and mother did not deliberately want him to become a tennis player. He had simply basked in this environment from a very young age, always at the courtside with his tennis-teacher mother and his father, a passionate spectator.

Praised at a very young age and supported by his parents who passed on their passion for sports, Jan developed a fabulous technique by copying the movements of players the moment he saw them.

After noticing how quickly this prodigy was progressing, his parents decided to turn him into a champion.

After noticing how quickly this prodigy was progressing, his parents decided to turn him into a champion and brought him to the Academy, even though he was only four years old. They then put into practice the essential aspects of a winning method.

Since their arrival in France, outraged commentary has come from all sides: too early, too young, always too, too, too...We are accused of disrupting the child's natural development, stunting his growth, manipulating the natural rate of progression, of turning him into a circus freak and who knows what else.

But why is Jan too young to launch himself into this adventure? He attends a French school and will be bilingual very quickly. He is crazy about tennis and has an obvious talent. He is spending his formative years in a place that completely corresponds to his aspirations. It would be disingenuous to claim that he can not blossom in this ideal environment. Should parents who are told that their child is gifted deny the obvious and barely commit to the project, or instead, should they try to take every opportunity they can? All children burn up energy when they play. In this case, we maintain the fun side and Jan burns up his energy within a rationalized, supervised framework that sidesteps the traps found in amateur institutions.

Even though he started out more purposefully and earlier than others, he will not grow tired of playing tennis. The skeptics retort that immersing such a young child into the tennis world can only lead to burn-out and exhaustion.

But I would like people to give me concrete examples. I have lived on a tennis court for thirty years and have never gotten tired of it. How can you get bored when you're living out your passion? Jan could one day tire of tennis if it were made to be a burden. To avoid this, it will depend on how his teachers go about it.

Basically, we must always ensure that the child takes pleasure on the court, in the same way that we teach a child to read or to count in short sequences based on games or drawings. You have to be creative and always have the child's best interests in mind. With Jan, the sessions last between sixty and ninety minutes. It all depends on whether he has had a good nap or

Jan is constantly improving his coordination and rapidly starting to understand the difference between winning and losing.

not. He is at an age where everything is acquired very quickly. It is unthinkable not to capitalize on his formidable potential. By playing points or matches, by learning how to play many types of game, Jan is constantly improving his coordination and rapidly starting to understand the difference between winning and losing. These notions have become familiar to him very early. What a plus...

The main difficulty that had to be addressed was the family's adaptation to life in France. They were far away from their friends, living in another climate, at a different rhythm, in a different culture, and surrounded by a language they did not master. It took them a year to become acclimated. A year during which Jan unconsciously felt guilty seeing his family unhappy in Paris "because of him". Today, luckily, each family member has rediscovered their balance and Jan is progressing very quickly. His older brother, Kadyn, who was initially withdrawn, also shows great tennis skills. Furthermore, he serves as a model for Jan, and they are stronger together.

He seems to be exceptional. And he is, but only because he has never been set a single limit and because his entourage has given him self-belief. Everything else happened naturally...

Jan's education is that of a champion. His parents see unlimited potential in him. They are confident in the future despite the naysayers. Jan is developing extraordinary skills because of this. American TV shows fight over him because he is so gifted, and amazes people with his gifts. He seems to be exceptional. And he is, but only because he has never been set a single limit and because his entourage has given him self-belief. Everything else happened naturally...

EPILOGUE

I want to tell every parent that I know they are capable of applying the method successfully. It is by believing in the future and by advancing methodically that you prepare a child for a great life.

To summarize my method in a few words, I would say: Love and Availability; Positivity and Encouragement; Serenity and Determination.

Love and Availability. Positivity and Encouragement. Serenity and Determination.

In the numerous stories told here, the programming of players was very successful on some points and not so on others. Far from laying the blame with the parents, on the contrary, I notice with satisfaction that they often give everything they have: their love, their passion and their time. They sometimes achieve success, even if they do not always have the competence and the necessary method. Players develop their potential, but gray areas make their futures uncertain.

The coach's role is all the more important in such cases. If a player is accompanied correctly, he has a chance. He can succeed and capitalize on his potential, at least partially.

A true study must also be carried out in order to analyze their requirements and to find solutions. My professional approach proposes a "Team" for each high-level player; one that includes his inner circle, but also specialists who can help the player in every area.

...so that our players can fulfill their destinies and the smile of triumph on their faces will give us the feeling of a job well done.

As for us coaches, we must be armed with serenity, patience, enthusiasm and psychology; but also with strength and determination; because our profession requires us to be winners, so that our players can fulfill their destinies and the smile of triumph on their faces will give us the feeling of a job well done.

ACKNOWLEDGEMENTS

Thank you to Franck Ramella for your participation. Your help was precious to me. It allowed me to structure my thoughts.

Thank you to Mélanie De Truchis, my faithful proofreader. Your style helped me better understand what I wanted to say. Thank you for your time, your enthusiasm and your humor.

Thank you also to Carl Rodrigues, who was so considerate, so motivating, and so available. It is a pleasure to have you by my side professionally and as a friend.

Thank you to Karim Koulakssis for taking the time to always make intelligent remarks.

And thank you to my wife, Clarisse. It is also thanks to your support that I find the energy to launch myself into such projects.

Printed in Spain:

SAGRAFIC (Barcelona)

Photography credits

© ***Antonio Borga:*** *page 5 (photo 2) and page 10 (photo 2).*

Denis Boulanger* © *Éditions Amphora: *page 9 (photos 2 and 3).*

© ***Frédéric Chales:*** *page 2 (photos 1 and 3).*

Julien Crofnier and Antoine Couvercelle* © *Tennis Magazine: *page 3 (photos 1, 2 and 3) – page 6 (photos 1 and 2) – page 7 (photos 2 and 3) – page 8 (photo 1) – page 11 (photos 1 and 2) – page 12 (photo 1) – page 15 (photos 1 and 2) – page 16 (photo 1).*

© ***Sergio Giorgi:*** *page 8 (photo 2).*

© ***Icare photo:*** *page 10 (photo 1).*

© ***Clarisse Mouratoglou:*** *page 2 (photo 2) – page 4 - (photos 1, 2 and 3) – page 5 (photo 1) – page 7 (photo 1) – page 12 (photo 2) – page 13 (photos 1 and 2) – page 14 (photos 1 and 2).*

© ***Scott Silva:*** *page 9 (photo 1).*

© ***All Rights Reserved:*** *page 16 (photo 2).*

TEN YEARS OF SHARED PASSION

TRAINING SESSION WITH FIONA GERVAIS , CHAMPION OF THE FRENCH MINORS, AT THE ACADEMY IN MAY 2006.

AT THE 2007 AUSTRALIAN OPEN WITH GUILLAUME PEYRE, MARCOS BAGHDATIS' COACH.

TECHNICAL EXPLANATION TO CAMILA GIORGI, STRONG ITALIAN HOPEFUL, AND HER FATHER, SERGIO, IN MAY 2006.

THE MOURATOGLOU CLAN DURING THE BAGHDATIS/AGASSI MATCH AT THE 2006 U.S. OPEN.

2006 U.S. OPEN DURING IRENA PAVLOVIC'S JUNIOR MATCH.

WIMBLEDON 2006 WITH MY DAUGHTER, JULIETTE, DURING THE MARCOS BAGHDATIS/RAFAEL NADAL MATCH.

WIMBLEDON 2006 DURING A TRAINING SESSION WITH MARCOS BAGHDATIS.

TRAINING DEBRIEFING WITH MEHDI DAOUKI, AN ACADEMY COACH, IN DECEMBER 2006.

END OF 2004 DURING A BASIC TRAINING WITH MARCOS BAGHDATIS AND IRENA PAVLOVIC.

RENZO OLIVO, YOUNG ITALO-ARGENTINIAN HOPEFUL, AT THE 2006 ORANGE BOWL. DETERMINED.

MARCOS BAGHDATIS AFTER BEATING SÉBASTIEN GROSJEAN AT THE 2007 FRENCH OPEN.

ARAVANE REZAI AT WIMBLEDON IN 2006. SHE REACHES THE 3RD ROUND.

WITH ARAVANE AND HER FATHER, ARSALAN REZAÏ AT WIMBLEDON IN 2007.

IN MIAMI WITH JULIA VAKULENKO WHEN I STARTED WORKING WITH HER IN DECEMBER 2006.

JULIA VAKULENKO, AUSTRALIAN OPEN 2007.

JULIAN VAKULENKO, No.33 WTA (AS OF 05/28/07), AT THE MIAMI OPEN IN JANUARY 2007.

ANASTASIA PAVLYUCHENKOVA, 2005 WORLD JUNIOR CHAMPION, AT THE FRENCH OPEN.

JUNE 2006, CAMILA GIORGI, 16, AT THE CHARLEROI JUNIOR TOURNAMENT.

JAN SILVA, 4, DURING OUR FIRST MEETING AT THE ACADEMY IN JUNE 2006.

JUNE 2007, JAN IS 5 YEARS OLD. WHAT BALANCE!

JUNE 2007 AT THE ACADEMY. JAN "THE LION" WITH ALL HIS RAGE.

MOURATOGLOU TENNIS ACADEMY AT THIVERVAL-GRIGNON (78), 30KM FROM PARIS.

AT THE ACADEMY IN JUNE 2007.

MAY 2005, IRENA PAVLOVIC DURING THE FRENCH JUNIOR CHAMPIONSHIPS THAT SHE WILL GO ON TO WIN.

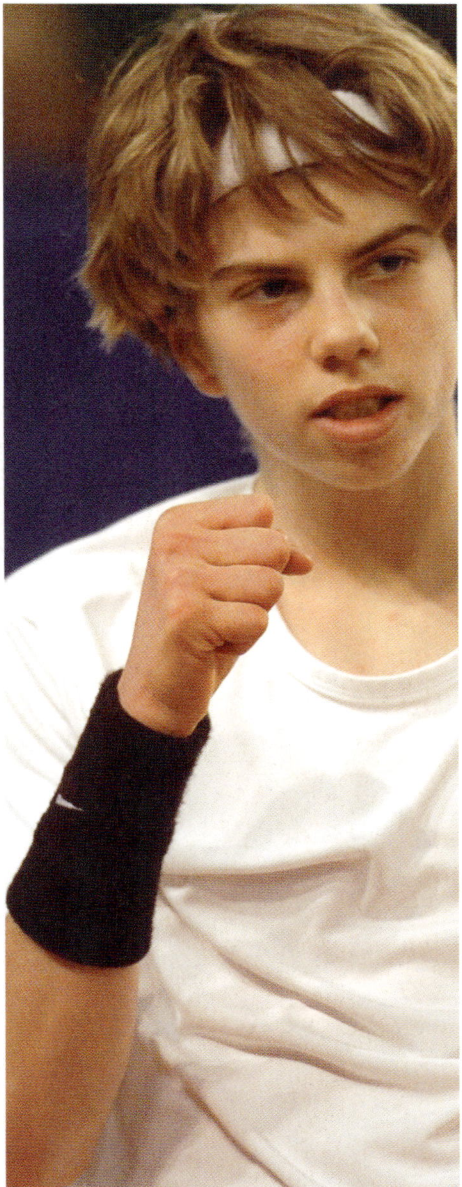

FEBRUARY 2006. SÉBASTIEN LAVIE REACHES THE FINAL OF THE “PETITS AS” TOURNAMENT IN TARBES.

MY GROUP DURING THE AWARDS CEREMONY AT THE 2006 AUSTRALIAN OPEN FINAL BAGHDATIS/FEDERER.

ORANGE BOWL 2006. MARCOS BAGHDATIS JUST WON THE FINAL.

MARCOS BAGHDATIS ON THE AUSTRALIAN OPEN OFFICIAL POSTER. A CONSECRATION!

MIAMI. DECEMBER 2003. MARCOS BAGHDATIS WINS THE ORANGE BOWL AND BECOMES WORLD JUNIOR CHAMPION.

MIAMI, MARCH 2007. WITH RICHARD WILLIAMS FOR A L'EQUIPE MAGAZINE ARTICLE.

U. S. OPEN 2005. TRAINING SESSION WITH MARCOS BAGHDATIS AND ANDRÉ AGASSI.

MARIO ANCIC DEFEATS ROGER FEDERER ON THE CENTER COURT AT WIMBLEDON 2003.

PAUL-HENRI MATHIEU, WINNER OF THE JUNIOR FRENCH OPEN, WHILE HE WAS TRAINING AT THE ACADEMY.

PAULINE PARMENTIER AT THE FRENCH OPEN. SHE WAS MY STUDENT FROM 15 TO 20 YEARS OLD.

GILLES MULLER, 2001 JUNIOR U.S. OPEN WINNER; IN DECEMBER HE WOULD BECOME JUNIOR WORLD CHAMPION.